CW00969272

PILLARS OF SOCIETY

Henrik Ibsen

Edition Published 2018
Edition edited by Saúl Arroyo and María Morgado
Cover art & design: Samuel Arroyo
Translated by R. Farquharson Sharp
ISBN-13: 978-1719353748
ISBN-10: 1719353743
 Printed by CreateSpace, An Amazon.com Company

Content

DRAMATIS PERSONAE

Karsten Bernick, a shipbuilder.
Mrs. Bernick, his wife.
Olaf, their son, thirteen years old.
Martha Bernick, Karsten Bernick's sister.
Johan Tonnesen, Mrs. Bernick's younger brother.
Lona Hessel, Mrs. Bernick's elder half-sister.
Hilmar Tonnesen, Mrs. Bernick's cousin.
Dina Dorf, a young girl living with the Bernicks.
Rorlund, a schoolmaster.
Rummel, a merchant.
Vigeland and Sandstad, tradesman
Krap, Bernick's confidential clerk.
Aune, foreman of Bernick's shipbuilding yard.
Mrs. Rummel.
Hilda Rummel, her daughter.
Mrs. Holt.
Netta Holt, her daughter.
Mrs. Lynge.

Townsfolk and visitors, foreign sailors, steamboat passengers, etc., etc.

(The action takes place at the Bernicks' house in one of the smaller coast towns in Norway)

ACT I.

(SCENE.--A spacious garden-room in the BERNICKS' house. In the foreground on the left is a door leading to BERNICK'S business room; farther back in the same wall, a similar door. In the middle of the opposite wall is a large entrance-door, which leads to the street. The wall in the background is almost wholly composed of plate-glass; a door in it opens upon a broad flight of steps which lead down to the garden; a sun-awning is stretched over the steps. Below the steps a part of the garden is visible, bordered by a fence with a small gate in it. On the other side of the fence runs a street, the opposite side of which is occupied by small wooden houses painted in bright colours. It is summer, and the sun is shining warmly. People are seen, every now and then, passing along the street and stopping to talk to one another; others going in and out of a shop at the corner, etc.

In the room a gathering of ladies is seated round a table. MRS. BERNICK is presiding; on her left side are MRS. HOLT and her daughter NETTA, and next to them MRS. RUMMEL and HILDA RUMMEL. On MRS. BERNICK'S right are MRS. LYNGE, MARTHA BERNICK and DINA DORF. All the ladies are busy working. On the table lie great piles of linen garments and other articles of clothing, some half finished, and some merely cut out. Farther back, at a small table on which two pots of flowers and a glass of sugared water are standing, RORLUND is sitting, reading aloud from a book with gilt edges, but only loud enough for the spectators to catch a word now and then. Out in the garden OLAF BERNICK is running about and shooting at a target with a toy crossbow.

After a moment AUNE comes in quietly through the door on the right. There is a slight interruption in the reading. MRS. BERNICK nods to him and points to the door on the left. AUNE goes quietly across, knocks softly at the door of BERNICK'S room, and after a moment's pause, knocks again. KRAP comes out of the room, with his hat in his hand and some papers under his arm.)

Krap: Oh, it was you knocking?

Aune: Mr. Bernick sent for me.

Krap: He did--but he cannot see you. He has deputed me to tell you--

Aune: Deputed you? All the same, I would much rather--

Krap: --deputed me to tell you what he wanted to say to you. You must give up these Saturday lectures of yours to the men.

Aune: Indeed? I supposed I might use my own time--

Krap: You must not use your own time in making the men useless in working hours. Last Saturday you were talking to them of the harm that would be done to the workmen by our new machines and the new working methods at the yard. What makes you do that?

Aune: I do it for the good of the community.

Krap: That's curious, because Mr. Bernick says it is disorganising the community.

Aune: My community is not Mr. Bernick's, Mr. Krap! As President of the Industrial Association, I must--

Krap: You are, first and foremost, President of Mr. Bernick's ship-building yard; and, before everything else, you have to do your duty to the community known as the firm of Bernick & Co.; that is what every one of us lives for. Well, now you know what Mr. Bernick had to say to you.

Aune: Mr. Bernick would not have put it that way, Mr. Krap! But I know well enough whom I have to thank for this. It is that damned American boat. Those fellows expect to get work done here the way they are accustomed to it over there, and that--

Krap: Yes, yes, but I can't go into all these details. You know now what Mr. Bernick means, and that is sufficient. Be so good as to go back to the yard; probably you are needed there. I shall be down myself in a little while. --Excuse me, ladies! (Bows to the ladies and goes out through the garden and down the street. AUNE goes quietly out to the right. RORLUND, who has continued his reading during the fore-going conversation, which has been carried on in low tones, has now come to the end of the book, and shuts it with a bang.)

Rorlund: There, my dear ladies, that is the end of it.

Mrs. Rummel: What an instructive tale!

Mrs. Holt: And such a good moral!

Mrs. Bernick: A book like that really gives one something to think about.

Rorlund: Quite so; it presents a salutary contrast to what, unfortunately, meets our eyes every day in the newspapers and magazines. Look at the gilded and painted exterior displayed by any large community, and think what it really conceals!--emptiness and rottenness, if I may say so; no foundation of morality beneath it. In a word, these large communities of ours now-a-days are whited sepulchres.

Mrs. Holt: How true! How true!

Mrs. Rummel: And for an example of it, we need look no farther than at the crew of the American ship that is lying here just now.

Rorlund: Oh, I would rather not speak of such offscourings of humanity as that. But even in higher circles--what is the case there? A spirit of doubt and unrest on all sides; minds never at peace, and instability characterising all their behaviour. Look how completely family life is undermined over there! Look at their shameless love of casting doubt on even the most serious truths!

Dina (without looking up from her work): But are there not many big things done there too?

Rorlund: Big things done--? I do not understand--.

Mrs. Holt (in amazement): Good gracious, Dina--!

Mrs. Rummel (in the same breath): Dina, how can you--?

Rorlund: I think it would scarcely be a good thing for us if such "big things" became the rule here. No, indeed, we ought to be only too thankful that things are as they are in this country. It is true enough that tares grow up amongst our wheat here too, alas; but we do our best conscientiously to weed them out as well as we are able. The important thing is to keep society pure, ladies--to ward off all the hazardous experiments that a restless age seeks to force upon us.

Mrs. Holt: And there are more than enough of them in the wind, unhappily.

Mrs. Rummel: Yes, you know last year we only by a hair's breadth escaped the project of having a railway here.

Mrs. Bernick: Ah, my husband prevented that.

Rorlund: Providence, Mrs. Bernick. You may be certain that your husband was the instrument of a higher Power when he refused to have anything to do with the scheme.

Mrs. Bernick: And yet they said such horrible things about him in the newspapers! But we have quite forgotten to thank you, Mr. Rorlund. It is really more than friendly of you to sacrifice so much of your time to us.

Rorlund: Not at all. This is holiday time, and--

Mrs. Bernick: Yes, but it is a sacrifice all the same, Mr. Rorlund.

Rorlund (drawing his chair nearer): Don't speak of it, my dear lady. Are you not all of you making some sacrifice in a good cause?--and that willingly and gladly? These poor fallen creatures for whose rescue we are working may be compared to soldiers wounded on the field of battle; you, ladies, are the kind-hearted sisters of mercy who prepare the lint for these stricken ones, lay the bandages softly on their wounds, heal them and cure them.

Mrs. Bernick: It must be a wonderful gift to be able to see everything in such a beautiful light.

Rorlund: A good deal of it is inborn in one--but it can be to a great extent acquired, too. All that is needful is to see things in the light of a serious mission in life. (To MARTHA:) What do you say, Miss Bernick? Have you not felt as if you were standing on firmer ground since you gave yourself up to your school work?

Martha: I really do not know what to say. There are times, when I am in the schoolroom down there, that I wish I were far away out on the stormy seas.

Rorlund: That is merely temptation, dear Miss Bernick. You ought to shut the doors of your mind upon such disturbing guests as that. By the "stormy seas"--for of course you do not intend me to take your words literally--you mean the restless tide of the great outer world, where so many are shipwrecked. Do you really set such store on the life you hear rushing by outside? Only look out into the street. There they go, walking about in the heat of the sun, perspiring and tumbling about over their little affairs. No, we undoubtedly have the best of it, who are able to sit here in the cool and turn our backs on the quarter from which disturbance comes.

Martha: Yes, I have no doubt you are perfectly right.

Rorlund: And in a house like this, in a good and pure home, where family life shows in its fairest colours--where peace and harmony rule-- (To MRS. BERNICK:) What are you listening to, Mrs. Bernick?

Mrs. Bernick (who has turned towards the door of BERNICK'S room): They are talking very loud in there.

Rorlund: Is there anything particular going on?

Mrs. Bernick: I don't know. I can hear that there is somebody with my husband.

(HILMAR TONNESEN, smoking a cigar, appears in the doorway on the right, but stops short at the sight of the company of ladies.)

Hilmar: Oh, excuse me-- (Turns to go back.)

Mrs. Bernick: No, Hilmar, come along in; you are not disturbing us. Do you want something?

Hilmar: No, I only wanted to look in here--Good morning, ladies. (To MRS. BERNICK:) Well, what is the result?

Mrs. Bernick: Of what?

Hilmar: Karsten has summoned a meeting, you know.

Mrs. Bernick: Has he? What about?

Hilmar: Oh, it is this railway nonsense over again.

Mrs. Rummel: Is it possible?

15

Mrs. Bernick: Poor Karsten, is he to have more annoyance over that?

Rorlund: But how do you explain that, Mr. Tonnesen? You know that last year Mr. Bernick made it perfectly clear that he would not have a railway here.

Hilmar: Yes, that is what I thought, too; but I met Krap, his confidential clerk, and he told me that the railway project had been taken up again, and that Mr. Bernick was in consultation with three of our local capitalists.

Mrs. Rummel: Ah, I was right in thinking I heard my husband's voice.

Hilmar: Of course Mr. Rummel is in it, and so are Sandstad and Michael Vigeland, "Saint Michael", as they call him.

Rorlund: Ahem!

Hilmar: I beg your pardon, Mr. Rorlund?

Mrs. Bernick: Just when everything was so nice and peaceful.

Hilmar: Well, as far as I am concerned, I have not the slightest objection to their beginning their squabbling again. It will be a little diversion, any way.

Rorlund: I think we can dispense with that sort of diversion.

Hilmar: It depends how you are constituted. Certain natures feel the lust of battle now and then. But unfortunately life in a country town does not offer much in that way, and it isn't given to every one to (turns the leaves of the book RORLUND has been reading). "Woman as the Handmaid of Society." What sort of drivel is this?

Mrs. Bernick: My dear Hilmar, you must not say that. You certainly have not read the book.

Hilmar: No, and I have no intention of reading it, either.

Mrs. Bernick: Surely you are not feeling quite well today.

Hilmar: No, I am not.

Mrs. Bernick: Perhaps you did not sleep well last night?

Hilmar: No, I slept very badly. I went for a walk yesterday evening for my health's sake; and I finished up at the club and read a book about a Polar expedition. There is something bracing in following the adventures of men who are battling with the elements.

Mrs. Rummel: But it does not appear to have done you much good, Mr. Tonnesen.

Hilmar: No, it certainly did not. I lay all night tossing about, only half asleep, and dreamt that I was being chased by a hideous walrus.

Olaf (who meanwhile has come up the steps from the garden): Have you been chased by a walrus, uncle?

Hilmar: I dreamt it, you duffer! Do you mean to say you are still playing about with that ridiculous bow? Why don't you get hold of a real gun?

Olaf: I should like to, but--

Hilmar: There is some sense in a thing like that; it is always an excitement every time you fire it off.

Olaf: And then I could shoot bears, uncle. But daddy won't let me.

Mrs. Bernick: You really mustn't put such ideas into his head, Hilmar.

Hilmar: Hm! It's a nice breed we are educating up now-a-days, isn't it! We talk a great deal about manly sports, goodness knows--but we only play with the question, all the same; there is never any serious inclination for the bracing discipline that lies in facing danger manfully. Don't stand pointing your crossbow at me, blockhead--it might go off!

Olaf: No, uncle, there is no arrow in it.

Hilmar: You don't know that there isn't--there may be, all the same. Take it away, I tell you!--Why on earth have you never gone over to America on one of your father's ships? You might have seen a buffalo hunt then, or a fight with Red Indians.

Mrs. Bernick: Oh, Hilmar--!

Olaf: I should like that awfully, uncle; and then perhaps I might meet Uncle Johan and Aunt Lona.

Hilmar: Hm!--Rubbish.

Mrs. Bernick: You can go down into the garden again now, Olaf.

Olaf: Mother, may I go out into the street too?

Mrs. Bernick: Yes, but not too far, mind.

(OLAF runs down into the garden and out through the gate in the fence.)

Rorlund: You ought not to put such fancies into the child's head, Mr. Tonnesen.

Hilmar: No, of course he is destined to be a miserable stay-at-home, like so many others.

Rorlund: But why do you not take a trip over there yourself?

Hilmar: I? With my wretched health? Of course I get no consideration on that account. But putting that out of the question, you forget that one has certain obligations to perform towards the community of which one forms a part. There must be some one here to hold aloft the banner of the Ideal.--Ugh, there he is shouting again!

The Ladies: Who is shouting?

Hilmar: I am sure I don't know. They are raising their voices so loud in there that it gets on my nerves.

Mrs. Bernick: I expect it is my husband, Mr. Tonnesen. But you must remember he is so accustomed to addressing large audiences.

Rorlund: I should not call the others low-voiced, either.

Hilmar: Good Lord, no!--not on any question that touches their pockets. Everything here ends in these petty material considerations. Ugh!

Mrs. Bernick: Anyway, that is a better state of things than it used to be when everything ended in mere frivolity.

Mrs. Lynge: Things really used to be as bad as that here?

Mrs. Rummel: Indeed they were, Mrs. Lynge. You may think yourself lucky that you did not live here then.

Mrs. Holt: Yes, times have changed, and no mistake, when I look back to the days when I was a girl.

Mrs. Rummel: Oh, you need not look back more than fourteen or fifteen years. God forgive us, what a life we led! There used to be a Dancing Society and a Musical Society--

Mrs. Bernick: And the Dramatic Club. I remember it very well.

Mrs. Rummel: Yes, that was where your play was performed, Mr. Tonnesen.

Hilmar (from the back of the room): What, what?

Rorlund: A play by Mr. Tonnesen?

Mrs. Rummel: Yes, it was long before you came here, Mr. Rorlund. And it was only performed once.

Mrs. Lynge: Was that not the play in which you told me you took the part of a young man's sweetheart, Mrs. Rummel?

Mrs. Rummel (glancing towards RORLUND): I? I really cannot remember, Mrs. Lynge. But I remember well all the riotous gaiety that used to go on.

Mrs. Holt: Yes, there were houses I could name in which two large dinner-parties were given in one week.

Mrs. Lynge: And surely I have heard that a touring theatrical company came here, too?

Mrs. Rummel: Yes, that was the worst thing of the lot.

Mrs. Holt (uneasily): Ahem!

Mrs. Rummel: Did you say a theatrical company? No, I don't remember that at all.

Mrs. Lynge: Oh yes, and I have been told they played all sorts of mad pranks. What is really the truth of those stories?

Mrs. Rummel: There is practically no truth in them, Mrs. Lynge.

Mrs. Holt: Dina, my love, will you give me that linen?

Mrs. Bernick (at the same time): Dina, dear, will you go and ask Katrine to bring us our coffee?

Martha: I will go with you, Dina. (DINA and MARTHA go out by the farther door on, the left.)

Mrs. Bernick (getting up): Will you excuse me for a few minutes? I think we will have our coffee outside. (She goes out to the verandah and sets to work to lay a table. RORLUND stands in the doorway talking to her. HILMAR sits outside, smoking.)

Mrs. Rummel (in a low voice): My goodness, Mrs. Lynge, how you frightened me!

Mrs. Lynge: I?

Mrs. Holt: Yes, but you know it was you that began it, Mrs. Rummel.

Mrs. Rummel: I? How can you say such a thing, Mrs. Holt? Not a syllable passed my lips!

Mrs. Lynge: But what does it all mean?

Mrs. Rummel: What made you begin to talk about--? Think--did you not see that Dina was in the room?

Mrs. Lynge: Dina? Good gracious, is there anything wrong with--?

Mrs. Holt: And in this house, too! Did you not know it was Mrs. Bernick's brother--?

Mrs. Lynge: What about him? I know nothing about it at all; I am quite new to the place, you know.

Mrs. Rummel: Have you not heard that--? Ahem! (To her daughter) Hilda, dear, you can go for a little stroll in the garden?

Mrs. Holt: You go too, Netta. And be very kind to poor Dina when she comes back. (HILDA and NETTA go out into the garden.)

Mrs. Lynge: Well, what about Mrs. Bernick's brother?

Mrs. Rummel: Don't you know the dreadful scandal about him?

Mrs. Lynge: A dreadful scandal about Mr. Tonnesen?

Mrs. Rummel: Good Heavens, no. Mr. Tonnesen is her cousin, of course, Mrs. Lynge. I am speaking of her brother--

Mrs. Holt: The wicked Mr. Tonnesen--

Mrs. Rummel: His name was Johan. He ran away to America.

Mrs. Holt: Had to run away, you must understand.

Mrs. Lynge: Then it is he the scandal is about?

Mrs. Rummel: Yes; there was something--how shall I put it?--there was something of some kind between him and Dina's mother. I remember it all as if it were yesterday. Johan Tonnesen was in old Mrs. Bernick's office then; Karsten Bernick had just come back from Paris-- he had not yet become engaged--

Mrs. Lynge: Yes, but what was the scandal?

Mrs. Rummel: Well, you must know that Moller's company were acting in the town that winter--

Mrs. Holt: And Dorf, the actor, and his wife were in the company. All the young men in the town were infatuated with her.

Mrs. Rummel: Yes, goodness knows how they could think her pretty. Well, Dorf came home late one evening--

Mrs. Holt: Quite unexpectedly.

Mrs. Rummel: And found his-- No, really it isn't a thing one can talk about.

Mrs. Holt: After all, Mrs. Rummel, he didn't find anything, because the door was locked on the inside.

Mrs. Rummel: Yes, that is just what I was going to say--he found the door locked. And--just think of it--the man that was in the house had to jump out of the window.

Mrs. Holt: Right down from an attic window.

Mrs. Lynge: And that was Mrs. Bernick's brother?

Mrs. Rummel: Yes, it was he.

Mrs. Lynge: And that was why he ran away to America?

Mrs. Holt: Yes, he had to run away, you may be sure.

Mrs. Rummel: Because something was discovered afterwards that was nearly as bad; just think--he had been making free with the cash-box...

Mrs. Holt: But, you know, no one was certain of that, Mrs. Rummel; perhaps there was no truth in the rumour.

Mrs. Rummel: Well, I must say--! Wasn't it known all over the town? Did not old Mrs. Bernick nearly go bankrupt as the result of it? However, God forbid I should be the one to spread such reports.

Mrs. Holt: Well, anyway, Mrs. Dorf didn't get the money, because she--

Mrs. Lynge: Yes, what happened to Dina's parents afterwards?

Mrs. Rummel: Well, Dorf deserted both his wife and his child. But madam was impudent enough to stay here a whole year. Of course she had not the face to appear at the theatre any more, but she kept herself by taking in washing and sewing--

Mrs. Holt: And then she tried to set up a dancing school.

Mrs. Rummel: Naturally that was no good. What parents would trust their children to such a woman? But it did not last very long. The fine madam was not accustomed to work; she got something wrong with her lungs and died of it.

Mrs. Lynge: What a horrible scandal!

Mrs. Rummel: Yes, you can imagine how hard it was upon the Bernicks. It is the dark spot among the sunshine of their good fortune, as Rummel once put it. So never speak about it in this house, Mrs. Lynge.

Mrs. Holt: And for heaven's sake never mention the stepsister, either!

Mrs. Lynge: Oh, so Mrs. Bernick has a step-sister, too?

22

Mrs. Rummel: Had, luckily-- for the relationship between them is all over now. She was an extraordinary person too! Would you believe it, she cut her hair short, and used to go about in men's boots in bad weather!

Mrs. Holt: And when her step-brother, the black sheep, had gone away, and the whole town naturally was talking about him--what do you think she did? She went out to America to him!

Mr. Rummel: Yes, but remember the scandal she caused before she went, Mrs. Holt.

Mrs. Holt: Hush, don't speak of it.

Mrs. Lynge: My goodness, did she create a scandal too?

Mrs. Rummel: I think you ought to hear it, Mrs. Lynge. Mr. Bernick had just got engaged to Betty Tonnesen, and the two of them went arm in arm into her aunt's room to tell her the news--

Mrs. Holt: The Tonnesens' parents were dead, you know--

Mrs. Rummel: When, suddenly, up got Lona Hessel from her chair and gave our refined and well-bred Karsten Bernick such a box on the ear that his head swam.

Mrs. Lynge: Well, I am sure I never--

Mrs. Holt: It is absolutely true.

Mrs. Rummel: And then she packed her box and went away to America.

Mrs. Lynge: I suppose she had had her eye on him for herself.

Mrs. Rummel: Of course she had. She imagined that he and she would make a match of it when he came back from Paris.

Mrs. Holt: The idea of her thinking such a thing! Karsten Bernick--a man of the world and the pink of courtesy, a perfect gentleman, the darling of all the ladies...

Mrs. Rummel: And, with it all, such an excellent young man, Mrs. Holt--so moral.

Mrs. Lynge: But what has this Miss Hessel made of herself in America?

Mrs. Rummel: Well, you see, over that (as my husband once put it) has been drawn a veil which one should hesitate to lift.

Mrs. Lynge: What do you mean?

Mrs. Rummel: She no longer has any connection with the family, as you may suppose; but this much the whole town knows, that she has sung for money in drinking saloons over there--

Mrs. Holt: And has given lectures in public--

Mrs. Rummel: And has published some mad kind of book.

Mrs. Lynge: You don't say so!

Mrs. Rummel: Yes, it is true enough that Lona Hessel is one of the spots on the sun of the Bernick family's good fortune. Well, now you know the whole story, Mrs. Lynge. I am sure I would never have spoken about it except to put you on your guard.

Mrs. Lynge: Oh, you may be sure I shall be most careful. But that poor child Dina Dorf! I am truly sorry for her.

Mrs. Rummel: Well, really it was a stroke of good luck for her. Think what it would have meant if she had been brought up by such parents! Of course we did our best for her, every one of us, and gave her all the good advice we could. Eventually Miss Bernick got her taken into this house.

Mrs. Holt: But she has always been a difficult child to deal with. It is only natural--with all the bad examples she had had before her. A girl of that sort is not like one of our own; one must be lenient with her.

Mrs. Rummel: Hush--here she comes. (In a louder voice.) Yes, Dina is really a clever girl. Oh, is that you, Dina? We are just putting away the things.

Mrs. Holt: How delicious your coffee smells, my dear Dina. A nice cup of coffee like that--

Mrs. Bernick (calling in from the verandah): Will you come out here? (Meanwhile MARTHA and DINA have helped the Maid to bring out the coffee. All the ladies seat themselves on the verandah, and talk with a great show of kindness to DINA. In a few moments DINA comes back into the room and looks for her sewing.)

Mrs. Bernick (from the coffee table): Dina, won't you--?

Dina: No, thank you. (Sits down to her sewing. MRS. BERNICK and RORLUND exchange a few words; a moment afterwards he comes back into the room, makes a pretext for going up to the table, and begins speaking to DINA in low tones.)

Rorlund: Dina.

Dina: Yes?

Rorlund: Why don't you want to sit with the others?

Dina: When I came in with the coffee, I could see from the strange lady's face that they had been talking about me.

Rorlund: But did you not see as well how agreeable she was to you out there?

Dina: That is just what I will not stand

Rorlund: You are very self-willed, Dina.

Dina: Yes.

Rorlund: But why?

Dina: Because it is my nature.

Rorlund: Could you not try to alter your nature?

Dina: No.

Rorlund: Why not?

Dina (looking at him): Because I am one of the "poor fallen creatures", you know.

Rorlund: For shame, Dina.

Dina: So was my mother.

Rorlund: Who has spoken to you about such things?

Dina: No one; they never do. Why don't they? They all handle me in such a gingerly fashion, as if they thought I should go to pieces if they---. Oh, how I hate all this kind-heartedness.

Rorlund: My dear Dina, I can quite understand that you feel repressed here, but--

Dina: Yes; if only I could get right away from here. I could make my own way quite well, if only I did not live amongst people who are so--so--

Rorlund: So what?

Dina: So proper and so moral.

Rorlund: Oh but, Dina, you don't mean that.

Dina: You know quite well in what sense I mean it. Hilda and Netta come here every day, to be exhibited to me as good examples. I can never be so beautifully behaved as they; I don't want to be. If only I were right away from it all, I should grow to be worth something.

Rorlund: But you are worth a great deal, Dina dear.

Dina: What good does that do me here?

Rorlund: Get right away, you say? Do you mean it seriously?

Dina: I would not stay here a day longer, if it were not for you.

Rorlund: Tell me, Dina--why is it that you are fond of being with me?

Dina: Because you teach me so much that is beautiful.

Rorlund: Beautiful? Do you call the little I can teach you, beautiful?

Dina: Yes. Or perhaps, to be accurate, it is not that you teach me anything; but when I listen to you talking I see beautiful visions.

Rorlund: What do you mean exactly when you call a thing beautiful?

Dina: I have never thought it out.

Rorlund: Think it out now, then. What do you understand by a beautiful thing?

26

Dina: A beautiful thing is something that is great--and far off.

Rorlund: Hm!--Dina, I am so deeply concerned about you, my dear.

Dina: Only that?

Rorlund: You know perfectly well that you are dearer to me than I can say.

Dina: If I were Hilda or Netta, you would not be afraid to let people see it.

Rorlund: Ah, Dina, you can have no idea of the number of things I am forced to take into consideration. When it is a man's lot to be a moral pillar of the community he lives in, he cannot be too circumspect. If only I could be certain that people would interpret my motives properly. But no matter for that; you must, and shall be, helped to raise yourself. Dina, is it a bargain between us that when I come-- when circumstances allow me to come--to you and say: "Here is my hand," you will take it and be my wife? Will you promise me that, Dina?

Dina: Yes.

Rorlund: Thank you, thank you! Because for my part, too--oh, Dina, I love you so dearly. Hush! Some one is coming. Dina--for my sake--go out to the others.(She goes out to the coffee table. At the same moment RUMMEL, SANDSTAD and VIGELAND come out of BERNICK'S room, followed by Bernick, who has a bundle of papers in his hand.)

Bernick: Well, then, the matter is settled.

Vigeland: Yes, I hope to goodness it is.

Rummel: It is settled, Bernick. A Norseman's word stands as firm as the rocks on Dovrefjeld, you know!

Bernick: And no one must falter, no one give way, no matter what opposition we meet with.

Rummel: We will stand or fall together, Bernick.

Hilmar (coming in from the verandah): Fall? If I may ask, isn't it the railway scheme that is going to fall?

Bernick: No, on the contrary, it is going to proceed--

Rummel: Full steam, Mr. Tonnesen.

Hilmar (coming nearer): Really?

Rorlund: How is that?

Mrs. Bernick (at the verandah door): Karsten, dear, what is it that--?

Bernick: My dear Betty, how can it interest you? (To the three men.) We must get out lists of subscribers, and the sooner the better. Obviously our four names must head the list. The positions we occupy in the community makes it our duty to make ourselves as prominent as possible in the affair.

Sandstad: Obviously, Mr. Bernick.

Rummel: The thing shall go through, Bernick; I swear it shall!

Bernick: Oh, I have not the least anticipation of failure. We must see that we work, each one among the circle of his own acquaintances; and if we can point to the fact that the scheme is exciting a lively interest in all ranks of society, then it stands to reason that our Municipal Corporation will have to contribute its share.

Mrs. Bernick: Karsten, you really must come out here and tell us--

Bernick: My dear Betty, it is an affair that does not concern ladies at all.

Hilmar: Then you are really going to support this railway scheme after all?

Bernick: Yes, naturally.

Rorlund: But last year, Mr. Bernick--

Bernick: Last year it was quite another thing. At that time it was a question of a line along the coast--

Vigeland: Which would have been quite superfluous, Mr. Rorlund; because, of course, we have our steamboat service--

Sandstad: And would have been quite unreasonably costly--

Rummel: Yes, and would have absolutely ruined certain important interests in the town.

Bernick: The main point was that it would not have been to the advantage of the community as a whole. That is why I opposed it, with the result that the inland line was resolved upon.

Hilmar: Yes, but surely that will not touch the towns about here.

Bernick: It will eventually touch our town, my dear Hilmar, because we are going to build a branch line here.

Hilmar: Aha--a new scheme, then?

Rummel: Yes, isn't it a capital scheme? What?

Rorlund: Hm!--

Vigeland: There is no denying that it looks as though Providence had just planned the configuration of the country to suit a branch line.

Rorlund: Do you really mean it, Mr. Vigeland?

Bernick: Yes, I must confess it seems to me as if it had been the hand of Providence that caused me to take a journey on business this spring, in the course of which I happened to traverse a valley through which I had never been before. It came across my mind like a flash of lightning that this was where we could carry a branch line down to our town. I got an engineer to survey the neighbourhood, and have here the provisional calculations and estimate; so there is nothing to hinder us.

Mrs. Bernick (who is still with the other ladies at the verandah door): But, my dear Karsten, to think that you should have kept it all a secret from us!

Bernick: Ah, my dear Betty, I knew you would not have been able to grasp the exact situation. Besides, I have not mentioned it to a living soul until today. But now the decisive moment has come, and we must work openly and with all our might. Yes, even if I have to risk all I have for its sake, I mean to push the matter through.

Rummel: And we will back you up, Bernick; you may rely upon that.

Rorlund: Do you really promise us so much, then, from this undertaking, gentlemen?

Bernick: Yes, undoubtedly. Think what a lever it will be to raise the status of our whole community. Just think of the immense tracts of forest-land that it will make accessible; think of all the rich deposits of minerals we shall be able to work; think of the river with one waterfall above another! Think of the possibilities that open out in the way of manufactories!

Rorlund: And are you not afraid that an easier intercourse with the depravity of the outer world--?

Bernick: No, you may make your mind quite easy on that score, Mr. Rorlund. Our little hive of industry rests now-a-days, God be thanked, on such a sound moral basis; we have all of us helped to drain it, if I may use the expression; and that we will continue to do, each in his degree. You, Mr. Rorlund, will continue your richly blessed activity in our schools and our homes. We, the practical men of business, will be the support of the community by extending its welfare within as wide a radius as possible; and our women--yes, come nearer ladies-- you will like to hear it--our women, I say, our wives and daughters-- you, ladies--will work on undisturbed in the service of charity, and moreover will be a help and a comfort to your nearest and dearest, as my dear Betty and Martha are to me and Olaf.(Looks around him.) Where is Olaf today?

Mrs. Bernick: Oh, in the holidays it is impossible to keep him at home.

Bernick: I have no doubt he is down at the shore again. You will see he will end by coming to some harm there.

Hilmar: Bah! A little sport with the forces of nature

Mrs. Rummel: Your family affection is beautiful, Mr. Bernick!

Bernick: Well, the family is the kernel of society. A good home, honoured and trusty friends, a little snug family circle where no disturbing elements can cast their shadow-- (KRAP comes in from the right, bringing letters and papers.)

Krap: The foreign mail, Mr. Bernick--and a telegram from New York.

30

Bernick (taking the telegram): Ah--from the owners of the "Indian Girl".

Rummel: Is the mail in? Oh, then you must excuse me.

Vigeland: And me too.

Sandstad: Good day, Mr. Bernick.

Bernick: Good day, good day, gentlemen. And remember, we have a meeting this afternoon at five o'clock.

The Three Men: Yes--quite so--of course. (They go out to the right.)

Bernick (who has read the telegram): This is thoroughly American! Absolutely shocking!

Mrs. Bernick: Good gracious, Karsten, what is it?

Bernick: Look at this, Krap! Read it!

Krap (reading): "Do the least repairs possible. Send over 'Indian Girl' as soon as she is ready to sail; good time of year; at a pinch her cargo will keep her afloat." Well, I must say--

Rorlund: You see the state of things in these vaunted great communities!

Bernick: You are quite right; not a moment's consideration for human life, when it is a question of making a profit. (To KRAP:) Can the "Indian Girl" go to sea in four--or five--days?

Krap: Yes, if Mr. Vigeland will agree to our stopping work on the "Palm Tree" meanwhile.

Bernick: Hm--he won't. Well, be so good as to look through the letters. And look here, did you see Olaf down at the quay?

Krap: No, Mr. Bernick. (Goes into BERNICK'S room.)

Bernick (looking at the telegram again): These gentlemen think nothing of risking eight men's lives--

Hilmar: Well, it is a sailor's calling to brave the elements; it must be a fine tonic to the nerves to be like that, with only a thin plank between one and the abyss--

Bernick: I should like to see the ship-owner amongst us who would condescend to such a thing! There is not one that would do it--not a single one! (Sees OLAF coming up to the house.) Ah, thank Heaven, here he is, safe and sound. (OLAF, with a fishing-line in his hand, comes running up the garden and in through the verandah.)

Olaf: Uncle Hilmar, I have been down and seen the steamer.

Bernick: Have you been down to the quay again?

Olaf: No, I have only been out in a boat. But just think, Uncle Hilmar, a whole circus company has come on shore, with horses and animals; and there were such lots of passengers.

Mrs. Rummel: No, are we really to have a circus?

Rorlund: We? I certainly have no desire to see it.

Mrs. Rummel: No, of course I don't mean we, but--

Dina: I should like to see a circus very much.

Olaf: So should I.

Hilmar: You are a duffer. Is that anything to see? Mere tricks. No, it would be something quite different to see the Gaucho careering over the Pampas on his snorting mustang. But, Heaven help us, in these wretched little towns of ours.

Olaf (pulling at MARTHA'S dress): Look, Aunt Martha! Look, there they come!

Mrs. Holt: Good Lord, yes--here they come.

Mrs. Lynge: Ugh, what horrid people!

(A number of passengers and a whole crowd of townsfolk, are seen coming up the street.)

Mrs. Rummel: They are a set of mountebanks, certainly. Just look at that woman in the grey dress, Mrs. Holt--the one with a knapsack over her shoulder.

Mrs. Holt: Yes--look--she has slung it on the handle of her parasol. The manager's wife, I expect.

32

Mrs. Rummel: And there is the manager himself, no doubt. He looks a regular pirate. Don't look at him, Hilda!

Mrs. Holt: Nor you, Netta!

Olaf: Mother, the manager is bowing to us.

Bernick: What?

Mrs. Bernick: What are you saying, child?

Mrs. Rummel: Yes, and--good Heavens--the woman is bowing to us too.

Bernick: That is a little too cool--

Martha (exclaims involuntarily): Ah--!

Mrs. Bernick: What is it, Martha?

Martha: Nothing, nothing. I thought for a moment--

Olaf (shrieking with delight): Look, look, there are the rest of them, with the horses and animals! And there are the Americans, too! All the sailors from the "Indian Girl"! (The strains of "Yankee Doodle," played on a clarinet and a drum, are heard.)

Hilmar (stopping his ears): Ugh, ugh, ugh!

Rorlund: I think we ought to withdraw ourselves from sight a little, ladies; we have nothing to do with such goings on. Let us go to our work again.

Mrs. Bernick: Do you think we had better draw the curtains?

Rorlund: Yes, that was exactly what I meant.

(The ladies resume their places at the work-table; RORLUND shuts the verandah door, and draws the curtains over it and over the windows, so that the room becomes half dark.)

Olaf (peeping out through the curtains): Mother, the manager's wife is standing by the fountain now, washing her face.

Mrs. Bernick: What? In the middle of the marketplace?

Mrs. Rummel: And in broad daylight, too!

Hilmar: Well, I must say if I were travelling across a desert waste and found myself beside a well, I am sure I should not stop to think whether--. Ugh, that frightful clarinet!

Rorlund: It is really high time the police interfered.

Bernick: Oh no; we must not be too hard on foreigners. Of course these folk have none of the deep-seated instincts of decency which restrain us within proper bounds. Suppose they do behave outrageously, what does it concern us? Fortunately this spirit of disorder, that flies in the face of all that is customary and right, is absolutely a stranger to our community, if I may say so--. What is this! (LONA HESSEL walks briskly in from the door on the right.)

The Ladies (in low, frightened tones): The circus woman! The manager's wife!

Mrs. Bernick: Heavens, what does this mean?

Martha (jumping up): Ah--!

Lona: How do you do, Betty dear! How do you do, Martha! How do you do, brother-in-law!

Mrs. Bernick (with a cry): Lona--!

Bernick (stumbling backwards): As sure as I am alive--!

Mrs. Holt: Mercy on us--!

Mrs. Rummel: It cannot possibly be--!

Hilmar: Well! Ugh!

Mrs. Bernick: Lona--! Is it really--?

Lona: Really me? Yes, indeed it is; you may fall on my neck if you like.

Hilmar: Ugh, ugh!

Mrs. Bernick: And coming back here as--?

Mrs. Bernick: And actually mean to appear in--?

Lona: Appear? Appear in what?

Bernick: Well, I mean--in the circus--

34

Lona: Ha, ha, ha! Are you mad, brother-in-law? Do you think I belong to the circus troupe? No, certainly I have turned my hand to a good many things and made a fool of myself in a good many ways--

Mrs. Rummel: Hm!

Lona: But I have never tried circus riding.

Bernick: Then you are not--?

Mrs. Bernick: Thank Heaven!

Lona: No, we travelled like other respectable folk, second-class, certainly, but we are accustomed to that.

Mrs. Bernick: We, did you say?

Bernick (taking a step for-ward): Whom do you mean by "we"?

Lona: I and the child, of course.

The Ladies (with a cry): The child!

Hilmar: What?

Rorlund: I really must say--!

Mrs. Bernick: But what do you mean, Lona?

Lona: I mean John, of course; I have no other child, as far as I know, but John, or Johan as you used to call him.

Mrs. Bernick: Johan--

Mrs. Rummel (in an undertone to MRS. LYNGE): The scapegrace brother!

Bernick (hesitatingly): Is Johan with you?

Lona: Of course he is; I certainly would not come without him. Why do you look so tragical? And why are you sitting here in the gloom, sewing white things? There has not been a death in the family, has there?

Rorlund: Madam, you find yourself in the Society for Fallen Women.

Lona (half to herself): What? Can these nice, quiet-looking ladies possibly be--?

Mrs. Rummel: Well, really--!

Lona: Oh, I understand! But, bless my soul, that is surely Mrs. Rummel? And Mrs. Holt sitting there too! Well, we three have not grown younger since the last time we met. But listen now, good people; let the Fallen Women wait for a day--they will be none the worse for that. A joyful occasion like this--

Rorlund: A home-coming is not always a joyful occasion.

Lona: Indeed? How do you read your Bible, Mr. Parson?

Rorlund: I am not a parson.

Lona: Oh, you will grow into one, then. But--faugh!--this moral linen of yours smells tainted, just like a winding-sheet. I am accustomed to the air of the prairies, let me tell you.

Bernick (wiping his forehead): Yes, it certainly is rather close in here.

Lona: Wait a moment; we will resurrect ourselves from this vault. (Pulls the curtains to one side) We must have broad daylight in here when the boy comes. Ah, you will see a boy then that has washed himself.

Hilmar: Ugh!

Lona (opening the verandah door and window): I should say, when he has washed himself, up at the hotel--for on the boat he got piggishly dirty.

Hilmar: Ugh, ugh!

Lona: Ugh? Why, surely isn't that--? (Points at HILDAR and asks the others): Is he still loafing about here saying "Ugh"?

Hilmar: I do not loaf; it is the state of my health that keeps me here.

Rorlund: Ahem! Ladies, I do not think--

Lona (who has noticed OLAF): Is he yours, Betty? Give me a paw, my boy! Or are you afraid of your ugly old aunt?

Rorlund (putting his book under his arm): Ladies, I do not think any of us is in the mood for any more work today. I suppose we are to meet again tomorrow?

Lona (while the others are getting up and taking their leave): Yes, let us. I shall be on the spot.

Rorlund: You? Pardon me, Miss Hessel, but what do you propose to do in our Society?

Lona: I will let some fresh air into it, Mr. Parson.

ACT II

(SCENE.--The same room. MRS. BERNICK is sitting alone at the work-table, sewing. BERNICK comes in from the right, wearing his hat and gloves and carrying a stick.)

Mrs. Bernick: Home already, Karsten?

Bernick: Yes, I have made an appointment with a man.

Mrs. Bernick (with a sigh): Oh yes, I suppose Johan is coming up here again.

Bernick: With a man, I said. (Lays down his hat.) What has become of all the ladies today?

Mrs. Bernick: Mrs. Rummel and Hilda hadn't time to come.

Bernick: Oh!--did they send any excuse?

Mrs. Bernick: Yes, they had so much to do at home.

Bernick: Naturally. And of course the others are not coming either?

Mrs. Bernick: No, something has prevented them today, too.

Bernick: I could have told you that, beforehand. Where is Olaf?

Mrs. Bernick: I let him go out a little with Dina.

Bernick: Hm--she is a giddy little baggage. Did you see how she at once started making a fuss of Johan yesterday?

Mrs. Bernick: But, my dear Karsten, you know Dina knows nothing whatever of--

Bernick: No, but in any case Johan ought to have had sufficient tact not to pay her any attention. I saw quite well, from his face, what Vigeland thought of it.

Mrs. Bernick (laying her sewing down on her lap): Karsten, can you imagine what his objective is in coming here?

Bernick: Well--I know he has a farm over there, and I fancy he is not doing particularly well with it; she called attention yesterday to the fact that they were obliged to travel second class--

Mrs. Bernick: Yes, I am afraid it must be something of that sort. But to think of her coming with him! She! After the deadly insult she offered you!

Bernick: Oh, don't think about that ancient history.

Mrs. Bernick: How can I help thinking of it just now? After all, he is my brother--still, it is not on his account that I am distressed, but because of all the unpleasantness it would mean for you. Karsten, I am so dreadfully afraid!

Bernick: Afraid of what?

Mrs. Bernick: Isn't it possible that they may send him to prison for stealing that money from your mother?

Bernick: What rubbish! Who can prove that the money was stolen?

Mrs. Bernick: The whole town knows it, unfortunately; and you know you said yourself.

Bernick: I said nothing. The town knows nothing whatever about the affair; the whole thing was no more than idle rumour.

Mrs. Bernick: How magnanimous you are, Karsten!

Bernick: Do not let us have any more of these reminiscences, please! You don't know how you torture me by raking all that up. (Walks up and down; then flings his stick away from him.) And to think of their coming home now--just now, when it is particularly necessary for me that I should stand well in every respect with the town and with the Press. Our newspaper men will be sending paragraphs to the papers in the other towns about here. Whether I receive them well, or whether I receive them ill, it will all be discussed and talked over. They will rake up all those old stories--as you do. In a community like ours--(Throws his gloves down on the table.) And I have not a soul here to whom I can talk about it and to whom I can go for support.

Mrs. Bernick: No one at all, Karsten?

Bernick: No--who is there? And to have them on my shoulders just at this moment! Without a doubt they will create a scandal in some way or another--she, in particular. It is simply a calamity to be connected with such folk in any way!

Mrs. Bernick: Well, I can't help their--

Bernick: What can't you help? Their being your relations? No, that is quite true.

Mrs. Bernick: And I did not ask them to come home.

Bernick: That's it--go on! "I did not ask them to come home; I did not write to them; I did not drag them home by the hair of their heads!" Oh, I know the whole rigmarole by heart.

Mrs. Bernick (bursting into tears): You need not be so unkind--

Bernick: Yes, that's right--begin to cry, so that our neighbours may have that to gossip about too. Do stop being so foolish, Betty. Go and sit outside; some one may come in here. I don't suppose you want people to see the lady of the house with red eyes? It would be a nice thing, wouldn't it, if the story got out about that--. There, I hear some one in the passage. (A knock is heard at the door.) Come in! (MRS. BERNICK takes her sewing and goes out down the garden steps. AUNE comes in from the right.)

Aune: Good morning, Mr. Bernick.

Bernick: Good morning. Well, I suppose you can guess what I want you for?

Aune: Mr. Krap told me yesterday that you were not pleased with--

Bernick: I am displeased with the whole management of the yard, Aune. The work does not get on as quickly as it ought. The "Palm Tree" ought to have been under sail long ago. Mr. Vigeland comes here every day to complain about it; he is a difficult man to have with one as part owner.

Aune: The "Palm Tree" can go to sea the day after tomorrow.

Bernick: At last. But what about the American ship, the "Indian Girl," which has been laid up here for five weeks and--

Aune: The American ship? I understood that, before everything else, we were to work our hardest to get your own ship ready.

Bernick: I gave you no reason to think so. You ought to have pushed on as fast as possible with the work on the American ship also; but you have not.

Aune: Her bottom is completely rotten, Mr. Bernick; the more we patch it, the worse it gets.

Bernick: That is not the reason. Krap has told me the whole truth. You do not understand how to work the new machines I have provided-- or rather, you will not try to work them.

Aune: Mr. Bernick, I am well on in the fifties; and ever since I was a boy I have been accustomed to the old way of working--

Bernick: We cannot work that way now-a-days. You must not imagine, Aune, that it is for the sake of making profit; I do not need that, fortunately; but I owe consideration to the community I live in, and to the business I am at the head of. I must take the lead in progress, or there would never be any.

Aune: I welcome progress too, Mr. Bernick.

Bernick: Yes, for your own limited circle--for the working class. Oh, I know what a busy agitator you are; you make speeches, you stir people up; but when some concrete instance of progress presents itself-- as now, in the case of our machines--you do not want to have anything to do with it; you are afraid.

Aune: Yes, I really am afraid, Mr. Bernick. I am afraid for the number of men who will have the bread taken out of their mouths by these machines. You are very fond, sir, of talking about the consideration we owe to the community; it seems to me, however, that the community has its duties too. Why should science and capital venture to introduce these new discoveries into labour, before the community has had time to educate a generation up to using them?

Bernick: You read and think too much, Aune; it does you no good, and that is what makes you dissatisfied with your lot.

Aune: It is not, Mr. Bernick; but I cannot bear to see one good work-man dismissed after another, to starve because of these machines.

Bernick: Hm! When the art of printing was discovered, many a quill-driver was reduced to starvation.

Aune: Would you have admired the art so greatly if you had been a quill-driver in those days, sir?

Bernick: I did not send for you to argue with you. I sent for you to tell you that the "Indian Girl" must be ready to put to sea the day after tomorrow.

Aune: But, Mr. Bernick--

Bernick: The day after tomorrow, do you hear?--at the same time as our own ship, not an hour later. I have good reasons for hurrying on the work. Have you seen today's paper? Well, then you know the pranks these American sailors have been up to again. The rascally pack are turning the whole town upside down. Not a night passes without some brawling in the taverns or the streets--not to speak of other abominations.

Aune: Yes, they certainly are a bad lot.

Bernick: And who is it that has to bear the blame for all this disorder? It is I! Yes, it is I who have to suffer for it. These newspaper fellows are making all sorts of covert insinuations because we are devoting all our energies to the "Palm Tree." I, whose task in life it is to influence my fellow-citizens by the force of example, have to endure this sort of thing cast in my face. I am not going to stand that. I have no fancy for having my good name smirched in that way.

Aune: Your name stands high enough to endure that and a great deal more, sir.

Bernick: Not just now. At this particular moment I have need of all the respect and goodwill my fellow-citizens can give me. I have a big un-dertaking on, the stocks, as you probably have heard; but, if it should happen that evil-disposed persons succeeded in shaking the absolute confidence I enjoy, it might land me in the greatest difficulties. That is why I want, at any price, to avoid these shameful innuendoes in the papers, and that is why I name the day after tomorrow as the limit of the time I can give you.

Aune: Mr. Bernick, you might just as well name this afternoon as the limit.

Bernick: You mean that I am asking an impossibility?

Aune: Yes, with the hands we have now at the yard.

Bernick: Very good; then we must look about elsewhere.

Aune: Do you really mean, sir, to discharge still more of your old workmen?

Bernick: No, I am not thinking of that.

Aune: Because I think it would cause bad blood against you both among the townsfolk and in the papers, if you did that.

Bernick: Very probably; therefore, we will not do it. But, if the "Indian Girl" is not ready to sail the day after tomorrow, I shall discharge you.

Aune (with a start): Me! (He laughs.) You are joking, Mr. Bernick.

Bernick: I should not be so sure of that, if I were you.

Aune: Do you mean that you can contemplate discharging me?--Me, whose father and grandfather worked in your yard all their lives, as I have done myself--?

Bernick: Who is it that is forcing me to do it?

Aune: You are asking what is impossible, Mr. Bernick.

Bernick: Oh, where there's a will there's a way. Yes or no; give me a decisive answer, or consider yourself discharged on the spot.

Aune (coming a step nearer to him): Mr. Bernick, have you ever realised what discharging an old workman means? You think he can look about for another job? Oh, yes, he can do that; but does that dispose of the matter? You should just be there once, in the house of a workman who has been discharged, the evening he comes home bringing all his tools with him.

Bernick: Do you think I am discharging you with a light heart? Have I not always been a good master to you?

Aune: So much the worse, Mr. Bernick. Just for that very reason those at home will not blame you; they will say nothing to me, because they dare not; but they will look at me when I am not noticing, and think that I must have deserved it. You see, sir, that is--that is what I cannot bear. I am a mere nobody, I know; but I have always been accustomed to stand first in my own home. My humble home is a little community too, Mr. Bernick--a little community which I have been able to support and maintain because my wife has believed in me and because my children have believed in me. And now it is all to fall to pieces.

Bernick: Still, if there is nothing else for it, the lesser must go down before the greater; the individual must be sacrificed to the general welfare. I can give you no other answer; and that, and no other, is the way of the world. You are an obstinate man, Aune! You are opposing me, not because you cannot do otherwise, but because you will not exhibit 'the superiority of machinery over manual labour'.

Aune: And you will not be moved, Mr. Bernick, because you know that if you drive me away you will at all events have given the newspapers proof of your good will.

Bernick: And suppose that were so? I have told you what it means for me--either bringing the Press down on my back, or making them well-disposed to me at a moment when I am working for an objective which will mean the advancement of the general welfare. Well, then, can I do otherwise than as I am doing? The question, let me tell you, turns upon this--whether your home is to be supported, as you put it, or whether hundreds of new homes are to be prevented from existing--hundreds of homes that will never be built, never have a fire lighted on their hearth, unless I succeed in carrying through the scheme I am working for now. That is the reason why I have given you your choice.

Aune: Well, if that is the way things stand, I have nothing more to say.

Bernick: Hm--my dear Aune, I am extremely grieved to think that we are to part.

Aune: We are not going to part, Mr. Bernick.

44

Bernick: How is that?

Aune: Even a common man like myself has something he is bound to maintain.

Bernick: Quite so, quite so--then I presume you think you may promise--?

Aune: The "Indian Girl" shall be ready to sail the day after tomorrow. (Bows and goes out to the right.)

Bernick: Ah, I have got the better of that obstinate fellow! I take it as a good omen. (HILMAR comes in through the garden door, smoking a cigar.)

Hilmar (as he comes up the steps to the verandah): Good morning, Betty! Good morning, Karsten!

Mrs. Bernick: Good morning.

Hilmar: Ah, I see you have been crying, so I suppose you know all about it too?

Mrs. Bernick: Know all about what?

Hilmar: That the scandal is in full swing. Ugh!

Bernick: What do you mean?

Hilmar (coming into the room): Why, that our two friends from America are displaying themselves about the streets in the company of Dina Dorf.

Mrs. Bernick (coming in after him): Hilmar, is it possible?

Hilmar: Yes, unfortunately, it is quite true. Lona was even so wanting in tact as to call after me, but of course I appeared not to have heard her.

Bernick: And no doubt all this has not been unnoticed.

Hilmar: You may well say that. People stood still and looked at them. It spread like wildfire through the town--just like a prairie fire out West. In every house people were at the windows waiting for the procession to pass, cheek by jowl behind the curtains--ugh! Oh, you must excuse me, Betty, for saying "ugh"--this has got on my nerves. If it is going on, I shall be forced to think about getting right away from here.

Mrs. Bernick: But you should have spoken to him and represented to him that--

Hilmar: In the open street? No, excuse me, I could not do that. To think that the fellow should dare to show himself in the town at all! Well, we shall see if the Press doesn't put a stopper on him; yes--forgive me, Betty, but--

Bernick: The Press, do you say? Have you heard a hint of anything of the sort?

Hilmar: There are such things flying about. When I left here yesterday evening I looked in at the club, because I did not feel well. I saw at once, from the sudden silence that fell when I went in, that our American couple had been the subject of conversation. Then that impudent newspaper fellow, Hammer, came in and congratulated me at the top of his voice on the return of my rich cousin.

Bernick: Rich?

Hilmar: Those were his words. Naturally I looked him up and down in the manner he deserved, and gave him to understand that I knew nothing about Johan Tonnesen's being rich. "Really," he said, "that is very remarkable. People usually get on in America when they have something to start with, and I believe your cousin did not go over there quite empty-handed."

Bernick: Hm--now will you oblige me by--

Mrs. Bernick (distressed): There, you see, Karsten!

Hilmar: Anyhow, I have spent a sleepless night because of them. And here he is, walking about the streets as if nothing were the matter. Why couldn't he disappear for good and all? It really is insufferable how hard some people are to kill.

Mrs. Bernick: My dear Hilmar, what are you saying P

Hilmar: Oh, nothing. But here this fellow escapes with a whole skin from railway accidents and fights with California grizzlies and Blackfoot Indians--has not even been scalped--. Ugh, here they come!

Bernick (looking down the street): Olaf is with them too!

Hilmar: Of course! They want to remind everybody that they belong to the best family in the town. Look there!--look at the crowd of loafers that have come out of the chemist's to stare at them and make remarks. My nerves really won't stand it; how a man is to be expected to keep the banner of the Ideal flying under such circumstances, I--

Bernick: They are coming here. Listen, Betty; it is my particular wish that you should receive them in the friendliest possible way.

Mrs. Bernick: Oh, may I, Karsten.

Bernick: Certainly, certainly--and you too, Hilmar. It is to be hoped they will not stay here very long; and when we are quite by ourselves--no allusions to the past; we must not hurt their feelings in any way.

Mrs. Bernick: How magnanimous you are, Karsten!

Bernick: Oh, don't speak of that.

Mrs. Bernick: But you must let me thank you; and you must forgive me for being so hasty. I am sure you had every reason to--

Bernick: Don't talk about it, please.

Hilmar: Ugh!

(JOHAN TONNESEN and DINA come up through the garden, followed by LONA and OLAF.)

Lona: Good morning, dear people!

Johan: We have been out having a look round the old place, Karsten.

Bernick: So I hear. Greatly altered, is it not?

Lona: Mr. Bernick's great and good works everywhere. We have been up into the Recreation Ground you have presented to the town.

Bernick: Have you been there?

Lona: "The gift of Karsten Bernick," as it says over the gateway. You seem to be responsible for the whole place here.

Johan: Splendid ships you have got, too. I met my old schoolfellow, the captain of the "Palm Tree."

Lona: And you have built a new school-house too; and I hear that the town has to thank you for both the gas supply and the water supply.

Bernick: Well, one ought to work for the good of the community one lives in.

Lona: That is an excellent sentiment, brother-in-law, but it is a pleasure, all the same, to see how people appreciate you. I am not vain, I hope; but I could not resist reminding one or two of the people we talked to that we were relations of yours.

Hilmar: Ugh!

Lona: Do you say "ugh" to that?

Hilmar: No, I said "ahem."

Lona: Oh, poor chap, you may say that if you like. But are you all by yourselves today?

Bernick: Yes, we are by ourselves today.

Lona: Ah, yes, we met a couple of members of your Morality Society up at the market; they made out they were very busy. You and I have never had an opportunity for a good talk yet. Yesterday you had your three pioneers here, as well as the parson.

Hilmar: The schoolmaster.

Lona: I call him the parson. But now tell me what you think of my work during these fifteen years? Hasn't he grown a fine fellow? Who would recognise the madcap that ran away from home?

Hilmar: Hm!

Johan: Now, Lona, don't brag too much about me.

Lona: Well, I can tell you I am precious proud of him. Goodness knows it is about the only thing I have done in my life; but it does give me a sort of right to exist. When I think, Johan, how we two began over there with nothing but our four bare fists.

Hilmar: Hands.

Lona: I say fists; and they were dirty fists.

Hilmar: Ugh!

Lona: And empty, too.

Hilmar: Empty? Well, I must say--

Lona: What must you say?

Bernick: Ahem!

Hilmar: I must say--ugh! (Goes out through the garden.)

Lona: What is the matter with the man?

Bernick: Oh, do not take any notice of him; his nerves are rather upset just now. Would you not like to take a look at the garden? You have not been down there yet, and I have got an hour to spare.

Lona: With pleasure. I can tell you my thoughts have been with you in this garden many and many a time.

Mrs. Bernick: We have made a great many alterations there too, as you will see. (BERNICK, MRS. BERNICK, and LONA go down to the garden, where they are visible every now and then during the following scene.)

Olaf (coming to the verandah door): Uncle Hilmar, do you know what uncle Johan asked me? He asked me if I would go to America with him.

Hilmar: You, you duffer, who are tied to your mother's apron strings--!

Olaf: Ah, but I won't be that any longer. You will see, when I grow big.

Hilmar: Oh, fiddlesticks! You have no really serious bent towards the strength of character necessary to--.

(They go down to the garden. DINA meanwhile has taken off her hat and is standing at the door on the right, shaking the dust off her dress.)

Johan (to DINA): The walk has made you pretty warm.

Dina: Yes, it was a splendid walk. I have never had such a splendid walk before.

Johan: Do you not often go for a walk in the morning?

Dina: Oh, yes--but only with Olaf.

Johan: I see.--Would you rather go down into the garden than stay here?

Dina: No, I would rather stay here.

Johan: So would I. Then shall we consider it a bargain that we are to go for a walk like this together every morning?

Dina: No, Mr. Tonnesen, you mustn't do that.

Johan: What mustn't I do? You promised, you know.

Dina: Yes, but--on second thought--you mustn't go out with me.

Johan: But why not?

Dina: Of course, you are a stranger--you cannot understand; but I must tell you--

Johan: Well?

Dina: No, I would rather not talk about it.

Johan: Oh, but you must; you can talk to me about whatever you like.

Dina: Well, I must tell you that I am not like the other young girls here. There is something--something or other about me. That is why you mustn't.

Johan: But I do not understand anything about it. You have not done anything wrong?

Dina: No, not I, but--no, I am not going to talk any more about it now. You will hear about it from the others, sure enough.

50

Johan: Hm!

Dina: But there is something else I want very much to ask you.

Johan: What is that?

Dina: I suppose it is easy to make a position for oneself over in America?

Johan: No, it is not always easy; at first you often have to rough it and work very hard.

Dina: I should be quite ready to do that.

Johan: You?

Dina: I can work now; I am strong and healthy; and Aunt Martha taught me a lot.

Johan: Well, hang it, come back with us!

Dina: Ah, now you are only making fun of me; you said that to Olaf too. But what I wanted to know is if people are so very--so very moral over there?

Johan: Moral?

Dina: Yes; I mean are they as--as proper and as well-behaved as they are here?

Johan: Well, at all events they are not so bad as people here make out. You need not be afraid on that score.

Dina: You don't understand me. What I want to hear is just that they are not so proper and so moral.

Johan: Not? What would you wish them to be, then?

Dina: I would wish them to be natural.

Johan: Well, I believe that is just what they are.

Dina: Because in that case I should get on if I went there.

Johan: You would, for certain!--and that is why you must come back with us.

Dina: No, I don't want to go with you; I must go alone. Oh, I would make something of my life; I would get on--

Bernick (speaking to LONA and his wife at the foot of the garden steps): Wait a moment--I will fetch it, Betty dear; you might so easily catch cold. (Comes into the room and looks for his wife's shawl.)

Mrs. Bernick (from outside): You must come out too, Johan; we are going down to the grotto.

Bernick: No, I want Johan to stay here. Look here, Dina; you take my wife's shawl and go with them. Johan is going to stay here with me, Betty dear. I want to hear how he is getting on over there.

Mrs. Bernick: Very well--then you will follow us; you know where you will find us. (MRS. BERNICK, LONA and DINA go out through the garden, to the left. BERNICK looks after them for a moment, then goes to the farther door on the left and locks it, after which he goes up to JOHAN, grasps both his hands, and shakes them warmly.)

Bernick: Johan, now that we are alone, you must let me thank you.

Johan: Oh, nonsense!

Bernick: My home and all the happiness that it means to me--my position here as a citizen--all these I owe to you.

Johan: Well, I am glad of it, Karsten; some good came of that mad story after all, then.

Bernick (grasping his hands again): But still you must let me thank you! Not one in ten thousand would have done what you did for me.

Johan: Rubbish! Weren't we, both of us, young and thoughtless? One of us had to take the blame, you know.

Bernick: But surely the guilty one was the proper one to do that?

Johan: Stop! At the moment the innocent one happened to be the proper one to do it. Remember, I had no ties--I was an orphan; it was a lucky chance to get free from the drudgery of the office. You, on the other hand, had your old mother still alive; and, besides that, you had just become secretly engaged to Betty, who was devoted to you. What would have happened between you and her if it had come to her ears?

Bernick: That is true enough, but still--

Johan: And wasn't it just for Betty's sake that you broke off your acquaintance with Mrs. Dorf? Why, it was merely in order to put an end to the whole thing that you were up there with her that evening.

Bernick: Yes, that unfortunate evening when that drunken creature came home! Yes, Johan, it was for Betty's sake; but, all the same, it was splendid of you to let all the appearances go against you, and to go away.

Johan: Put your scruples to rest, my dear Karsten. We agreed that it should be so; you had to be saved, and you were my friend. I can tell you, I was uncommonly proud of that friendship. Here was I, drudging away like a miserable stick-in-the-mud, when you came back from your grand tour abroad, a great swell who had been to London and to Paris; and you chose me for your chum, although I was four years younger than you--it is true it was because you were courting Betty, I understand that now--but I was proud of it! Who would not have been? Who would not willingly have sacrificed himself for you?--especially as it only meant a month's talk in the town, and enabled me to get away into the wide world.

Bernick: Ah, my dear Johan, I must be candid and tell you that the story is not so completely forgotten yet.

Johan: Isn't it? Well, what does that matter to me, once I am back over there on my farm again?

Bernick: Then you mean to go back?

Johan: Of course.

Bernick: But not immediately, I hope?

Johan: As soon as possible. It was only to humour Lona that I came over with her, you know.

Bernick: Really? How so?

Johan: Well, you see, Lona is no longer young, and lately she began to be obsessed with home-sickness; but she never would admit it.

(Smiles.) How could she venture to risk leaving such a flighty fellow as me alone, who before I was nineteen had been mixed up in...

Bernick: Well, what then?

Johan: Well, Karsten, now I am coming to a confession that I am ashamed to make.

Bernick: You surely haven't confided the truth to her?

Johan: Yes. It was wrong of me, but I could not do otherwise. You can have no conception what Lona has been to me. You never could put up with her; but she has been like a mother to me. The first year we were out there, when things went so badly with us, you have no idea how she worked! And when I was ill for a long time, and could earn nothing and could not prevent her, she took to singing ballads in taverns, and gave lectures that people laughed at; and then she wrote a book that she has both laughed and cried over since then--all to keep the life in me. Could I look on when in the winter she, who had toiled and drudged for me, began to pine away? No, Karsten, I couldn't. And so I said, "You go home for a trip, Lona; don't be afraid for me, I am not so flighty as you think." And so--the end of it was that she had to know.

Bernick: And how did she take it?

Johan: Well, she thought, as was true, that as I knew I was innocent nothing need prevent me from taking a trip over here with her. But make your mind easy; Lona will let nothing out, and I shall keep my mouth shut as I did before.

Bernick: Yes, yes I rely on that.

Johan: Here is my hand on it. And now we will say no more about that old story; luckily it is the only mad prank either of us has been guilty of, I am sure. I want thoroughly to enjoy the few days I shall stay here. You cannot think what a delightful walk we had this morning. Who would have believed that that little imp, who used to run about here and play angels' parts on the stage--! But tell me, my dear fellow, what became of her parents afterwards?

Bernick: Oh, my boy, I can tell you no more than I wrote to you immediately after you went away. I suppose you got my two letters?

Johan: Yes, yes, I have them both. So that drunken fellow deserted her?

Bernick: And drank himself to death afterwards.

Johan: And she died soon afterwards, too?

Bernick: She was proud; she betrayed nothing, and would accept nothing.

Johan: Well, at all events you did the right thing by taking Dina into your house.

Bernick: I suppose so. As a matter of fact it was Martha that brought that about.

Johan: So it was Martha? By the way, where is she today?

Bernick: She? Oh, when she hasn't her school to look after, she has her sick people to see to.

Johan: So it was Martha who interested herself in her.

Bernick: Yes, you know Martha has always had a certain liking for teaching; so she took a post in the boarding-school. It was very ridiculous of her.

Johan: I thought she looked very worn yesterday; I should be afraid her health was not good enough for it.

Bernick: Oh, as far as her health goes, it is all right enough. But it is unpleasant for me; it looks as though I, her brother, were not willing to support her.

Johan: Support her? I thought she had means enough of her own.

Bernick: Not a penny. Surely you remember how badly off our mother was when you went away? She carried things on for a time with my assistance, but naturally I could not put up with that state of affairs permanently. I made her take me into the firm, but even then things did not go well. So I had to take over the whole business myself, and when we made up our balance-sheet, it became evident that there was

55

practically nothing left as my mother's share. And when mother died soon afterwards, of course Martha was left penniless.

Johan: Poor Martha!

Bernick: Poor! Why? You surely do not suppose I let her want for anything? No, I venture to say I am a good brother. Of course she has a home here with us; her salary as a teacher is more than enough for her to dress on; what more could she want?

Johan: Hm--that is not our idea of things in America.

Bernick: No, I dare say not--in such a revolutionary state of society as you find there. But in our small circle--in which, thank God, depravity has not gained a footing, up to now at all events--women are content to occupy a seemly, as well as modest, position. Moreover, it is Martha's own fault; I mean, she might have been provided for long ago, if she had wished.

Johan: You mean she might have married?

Bernick: Yes, and married very well, too. She has had several good offers--curiously enough, when you think that she is a poor girl, no longer young, and, besides, quite an insignificant person.

Johan: Insignificant?

Bernick: Oh, I am not blaming her for that. I most certainly would not wish her otherwise. I can tell you it is always a good thing to have a steady-going person like that in a big house like this--some one you can rely on in any contingency.

Johan: Yes, but what does she--?

Bernick: She? How? Oh well, of course she has plenty to interest herself in; she has Betty and Olaf and me. People should not think first of themselves--women least of all. We have all got some community, great or small, to work for. That is my principle, at all events. (Points to KRAP, who has come in from the right.) Ah, here is an example of it, ready to hand. Do you suppose that it is my own affairs that are absorbing me just now? By no means. (Eagerly to KRAP.) Well?

56

Krap (in an undertone, showing him a bundle of papers): Here are all the sale contracts, completed.

Bernick: Capital! Splendid!--Well, Johan, you must really excuse me for the present. (In a low voice, grasping his hand.) Thanks, Johan, thanks! And rest assured that anything I can do for you-- Well, of course you understand. Come along, Krap. (They go into BERNICK'S room.)

Johan (looking after them for a moment): Hm!-- (Turns to go down to the garden. At the same moment MARTHA comes in from the right, with a little basket over her arm.) Martha!

Martha: Ah, Johan--is it you?

Johan: Out so early?

Martha: Yes. Wait a moment; the others are just coming. (Moves towards the door on the left.)

Johan: Martha, are you always in such a hurry?

Martha: I?

Johan: Yesterday you seemed to avoid me, so that I never managed to have a word with you--we two old playfellows.

Martha: Ah, Johan; that is many, many years ago.

Johan: Good Lord--why, it is only fifteen years ago, no more and no less. Do you think I have changed so much?

Martha: You? Oh yes, you have changed too, although--

Johan: What do you mean?

Martha: Oh, nothing.

Johan: You do not seem to be very glad to see me again.

Martha: I have waited so long, Johan--too long.

Johan: Waited? For me to come?

Martha: Yes.

Johan. And why did you think I would come?

Martha: To atone for the wrong you had done.

Johan: I?

Martha: Have you forgotten that it was through you that a woman died in need and in shame? Have you forgotten that it was through you that the best years of a young girl's life were embittered?

Johan: And you can say such things to me? Martha, has your brother never--?

Martha: Never what?

Johan: Has he never--oh, of course, I mean has he never so much as said a word in my defence?

Martha: Ah, Johan, you know Karsten's high principles.

Johan: Hm--! Oh, of course; I know my old friend Karsten's high principles! But really this is--. Well, well. I was having a talk with him just now. He seems to me to have altered considerably.

Martha: How can you say that? I am sure Karsten has always been an excellent man.

Johan: Yes, that was not exactly what I meant--but never mind. Hm! Now I understand the light you have seen me in; it was the return of the prodigal that you were waiting for.

Martha: Johan, I will tell you what light I have seen you in. (Points down to the garden.) Do you see that girl playing on the grass down there with Olaf? That is Dina. Do you remember that incoherent letter you wrote me when you went away? You asked me to believe in you. I have believed in you, Johan. All the horrible things that were rumoured about you after you had gone must have been done through being led astray--from thoughtlessness, without premeditation.

Johan: What do you mean?

Martha: Oh! you understand me well enough--not a word more of that. But of course you had to go away and begin afresh--a new life. Your duties here which you never remembered to undertake--or never were able to undertake--I have undertaken for you. I tell you this, so that you shall not have that also to reproach yourself with. I have been a mother to that much-wronged child; I have brought her up as well as I was able.

Johan: And have wasted your whole life for that reason.

Martha: It has not been wasted. But you have come late, Johan.

Johan: Martha--if only I could tell you--. Well, at all events let me thank you for your loyal friendship.

Martha (with a sad smile): Hm.--Well, we have had it out now, Johan. Hush, some one is coming. Goodbye, I can't stay now. (Goes out through the farther door on the left. LONA comes in from the garden, followed by MRS. BERNICK.)

Mrs. Bernick: But good gracious, Lona--what are you thinking of?

Lona: Let me be, I tell you! I must and will speak to him.

Mrs. Bernick: But it would be a scandal of the worst sort! Ah, Johan-- still here?

Lona: Out with you, my boy; don't stay here in doors; go down into the garden and have a chat with Dina.

Johan: I was just thinking of doing so.

Mrs. Bernick: But--

Lona: Look here, Johan--have you had a good look at Dina?

Johan: I should think so!

Lona: Well, look at her to some purpose, my boy. That would be some-body for you!

Mrs. Bernick: But, Lona!

Johan: Somebody for me?

Lona: Yes, to look at, I mean. Be off with you!

Johan: Oh, I don't need any pressing. (Goes down into the garden.)

Mrs. Bernick: Lona, you astound me! You cannot possibly be serious about it?

Lona: Indeed I am. Isn't she sweet and healthy and honest? She is exactly the wife for Johan. She is just what he needs over there; it will be a change from an old step-sister.

Mrs. Bernick: Dina? Dina Dorf? But think--

Lona: I think first and foremost of the boy's happiness. Because, help him I must; he has not much idea of that sort of thing; he has never had much of an eye for girls or women.

Mrs. Bernick: He? Johan? Indeed I think we have had only too sad proofs that--

Lona: Oh, devil take all those stupid stories! Where is Karsten? I mean to speak to him.

Mrs. Bernick: Lona, you must not do it, I tell you.

Lona: I am going to. If the boy takes a fancy to her--and she to him-- then they shall make a match of it. Karsten is such a clever man, he must find some way to bring it about.

Mrs. Bernick: And do you think these American indecencies will be permitted here?

Lona: Bosh, Betty!

Mrs. Bernick: Do you think a man like Karsten, with his strictly moral way of thinking--

Lona: Pooh! he is not so terribly moral.

Mrs. Bernick: What have you the audacity to say?

Lona: I have the audacity to say that Karsten is not any more particularly moral than anybody else.

Mrs. Bernick: So you still hate him as deeply as that! But what are you doing here, if you have never been able to forget that? I cannot understand how you, dare look him in the face after the shameful insult you put upon him in the old days.

Lona: Yes, Betty, that time I did forget myself badly.

Mrs. Bernick: And to think how magnanimously he has forgiven you--he, who had never done any wrong! It was not his fault that you encouraged yourself with hopes. But since then you have always hated me too. (Bursts into tears.) You have always begrudged me my good fortune. And now you come here to heap all this on my head--to let the whole town know what sort of a family I have brought Karsten into. Yes, it is me that it all falls upon, and that is what you want. Oh, it is abominable of you! (Goes out by the door on the left, in tears.)

Lona (looking after her): Poor Betty! (BERNICK comes in from his room. He stops at the door to speak to KRAP.)

Bernick: Yes, that is excellent, Krap--capital! Send twenty pounds to the fund for dinners to the poor. (Turns round.) Lona! (Comes forward.) Are you alone? Is Betty not coming in?

Lona: No. Would you like me to call her?

Bernick: No, no--not at all. Oh, Lona, you don't know how anxious I have been to speak openly to you--after having begged for your forgiveness.

Lona: Look here, Karsten--do not let us be sentimental; it doesn't suit us.

Bernick: You must listen to me, Lona. I know only too well how much appearances are against me, as you have learnt all about that affair with Dina's mother. But I swear to you that it was only a temporary infatuation; I was really, truly and honestly, in love with you once.

Lona: Why do you think I have come home?

Bernick: Whatever you have in your mind, I entreat, you to do nothing until I have exculpated myself. I can do that, Lona; at all events I can excuse myself.

Lona: Now you are frightened. You once were in love with me, you say. Yes, you told me that often enough in your letters; and perhaps it was true, too--in a way--as long as you were living out in the great, free world which gave you the courage to think freely and greatly. Perhaps you found in me a little more character and strength of will and independence than in most of the folk at home here. And then we kept it secret between us; nobody could make fun of your bad taste.

Bernick: Lona, how can you think--?

Lona: But when you came back--when you heard the gibes that were made at me on all sides--when you noticed how people laughed at what they called my absurdities...

Bernick: You were regardless of people's opinion at that time.

Lona: Chiefly to annoy the petticoated and trousered prudes that one met at every turn in the town. And then, when you met that seductive young actress--

Bernick: It was a boyish escapade--nothing more; I swear to you that there was no truth in a tenth part of the rumours and gossip that went about.

Lona: Maybe. But then, when Betty came home--a pretty young girl, idolised by every one--and it became known that she would inherit all her aunt's money and that I would have nothing!

Bernick: That is just the point, Lona; and now you shall have the truth without any beating about the bush. I did not love Betty then; I did not break off my engagement with you because of any new attachment. It was entirely for the sake of the money. I needed it; I had to make sure of it.

Lona: And you have the face to tell me that?

Bernick: Yes, I have. Listen, Lona.

Lona: And yet you wrote to me that an unconquerable passion for Betty had overcome you--invoked my magnanimity--begged me, for Betty's sake, to hold my tongue about all that had been between us.

Bernick: I had to, I tell you.

Lona: Now, by Heaven, I don't regret that I forgot myself as I did that time--

Bernick: Let me tell you the plain truth of how things stood with me then. My mother, as you remember, was at the head of the business, but she was absolutely without any business ability whatever. I was hurriedly summoned home from Paris; times were critical, and they relied on me to set things straight. What did I find? I found--and you must keep this a profound secret--a house on the brink of ruin. Yes-- as good as on the brink of ruin, this old respected house which had seen three generations of us. What else could I--the son, the only son--do than look about for some means of saving it?

Lona: And so you saved the house of Bernick at the cost of a woman.

Bernick: You know quite well that Betty was in love with me.

Lona: But what about me?

Bernick: Believe me, Lona, you would never have been happy with me.

Lona: Was it out of consideration for my happiness that you sacrificed me?

Bernick: Do you suppose I acted as I did from selfish motives? If I had stood alone then, I would have begun all over again with cheerful courage. But you do not understand how the life of a man of business, with his tremendous responsibilities, is bound up with that of the business which falls to his inheritance. Do you realise that the prosperity or the ruin of hundreds--of thousands--depends on him? Can you not take into consideration the fact that the whole community in which both you and I were born would have been affected to the most dangerous extent if the house of Bernick had gone to smash?

Lon: Then is it for the sake of the community that you have maintained your position these fifteen years upon a lie?

Bernick: Upon a lie?

Lona: What does Betty know of all this...that underlies her union with you?

Bernick: Do you suppose that I would hurt her feelings to no purpose by disclosing the truth?

Lona: To no purpose, you say? Well, well--You are a man of business; you ought to understand what is to the purpose. But listen to me,

Karsten--I am going to speak the plain truth now. Tell me, are you really happy?

Bernick: In my family life, do you mean?

Lona: Yes.

Bernick: I am, Lona. You have not been a self-sacrificing friend to me in vain. I can honestly say that I have grown happier every year. Betty is good and willing; and if I were to tell you how, in the course of years, she has learned to model her character on the lines of my own--

Lona: Hm!

Bernick: At first, of course, she had a whole lot of romantic notions about love; she could not reconcile herself to the idea that, little by little, it must change into a quiet comradeship.

Lona: But now she is quite reconciled to that?

Bernick: Absolutely. As you can imagine, daily intercourse with me has had no small share in developing her character. Every one, in their degree, has to learn to lower their own pretensions, if they are to live worthily of the community to which they belong. And Betty, in her turn, has gradually learned to understand this; and that is why our home is now a model to our fellow citizens.

Lona: But your fellow citizens know nothing about the lie?

Bernick: The lie?

Lona: Yes--the lie you have persisted in for these fifteen years.

Bernick: Do you mean to say that you call that--?

Lona: I call it a lie--a threefold lie: first of all, there is the lie towards me; then, the lie towards Betty; and then, the lie towards Johan.

Bernick: Betty has never asked me to speak.

Lona: Because she has known nothing.

Bernick: And you will not demand it--out of consideration for her.

Lona: Oh, no--I shall manage to put up with their gibes well enough; I have broad shoulders.

Bernick: And Johan will not demand it either; he has promised me that.

Lona: But you yourself, Karsten? Do you feel within yourself no impulse urging you to shake yourself free of this lie?

Bernick: Do you suppose that of my own free will I would sacrifice my family happiness and my position in the world?

Lona: What right have you to the position you hold?

Bernick: Every day during these fifteen years I have earned some little right to it--by my conduct, and by what I have achieved by my work.

Lona: True, you have achieved a great deal by your work, for yourself as well as for others. You are the richest and most influential man in the town; nobody in it dares do otherwise than defer to your will, because you are looked upon as a man without spot or blemish; your home is regarded as a model home, and your conduct as a model of conduct. But all this grandeur, and you with it, is founded on a treacherous morass. A moment may come and a word may be spoken, when you and all your grandeur will be engulfed in the morass, if you do not save yourself in time.

Bernick: Lona--what is your object in coming here?

Lona: I want to help you to get firm ground under your feet, Karsten.

Bernick: Revenge!--you want to revenge yourself! I suspected it. But you won't succeed! There is only one person here that can speak with authority, and he will be silent.

Lona: You mean Johan?

Bernick: Yes, Johan. If any one else accuses me, I shall deny everything. If any one tries to crush me, I shall fight for my life. But you will never succeed in that, let me tell you! The one who could strike me down will say nothing--and is going away.

(RUMMEL and VIGELAND come in from the right.)

Rummel: Good morning, my dear Bernick, good morning. You must come up with us to the Commercial Association. There is a meeting about the railway scheme, you know.

Bernick: I cannot. It is impossible just now.

Vigeland: You really must, Mr. Bernick.

Rummel: Bernick, you must. There is an opposition to us on foot. Hammer, and the rest of those who believe in a line along the coast, are declaring that private interests are at the back of the new proposals.

Bernick: Well then, explain to them--

Vigeland: Our explanations have no effect, Mr. Bernick.

Rummel: No, no, you must come yourself. Naturally, no one would dare to suspect you of such duplicity.

Lona: I should think not.

Bernick: I cannot, I tell you; I am not well. Or, at all events, wait--let me pull myself together. (RORLUND comes in from the right.)

Rorlund: Excuse me, Mr. Bernick, but I am terribly upset.

Bernick: Why, what is the matter with you?

Rorlund. I must put a question to you, Mr. Bernick. Is it with your consent that the young girl who has found a shelter under your roof shows herself in the open street in the company of a person who--

Lona: What person, Mr. Parson?

Rorlund: With the person from whom, of all others in the world, she ought to be kept farthest apart!

Lona: Ha! ha!

Rorlund: Is it with your consent, Mr. Bernick?

Bernick (looking for his hat and gloves). I know nothing about it. You must excuse me; I am in a great hurry. I am due at the Commercial Association.

(HILMAR comes up from the garden and goes over to the farther door on the left.)

Hilmar: Betty--Betty, I want to speak to you.

Mrs. Bernick (coming to the door): What is it?

Hilmar: You ought to go down into the garden and put a stop to the flirtation that is going on between a certain person and Dina Dorf! It has quite got on my nerves to listen to them.

Lona: Indeed! And what has the certain person been saying?

Hilmar: Oh, only that he wishes she would go off to America with him. Ugh!

Rorlund: Is it possible?

Mrs. Bernick: What do you say?

Lona: But that would be perfectly splendid!

Bernick: Impossible! You cannot have heard right.

Hilmar: Ask him yourself, then. Here comes the pair of them. Only, leave me out of it, please.

Bernick (to RUMMEL and VIGELAND): I will follow you--in a moment. (RUMMEL and VIGELAND go out to the right. JOHAN and DINA come up from the garden.)

Johan: Hurrah, Lona, she is going with us!

Mrs. Bernick: But, Johan--are you out of your senses?

Rorlund: Can I believe my ears! Such an atrocious scandal! By what arts of seduction have you--?

Johan: Come, come, sir--what are you saying?

Rorlund: Answer me, Dina; do you mean to do this--entirely of your own free will?

Dina: I must get away from here.

Rorlund: But with him!--with him!

Dina: Can you tell me of any one else here who would have the courage to take me with him?

Rorlund: Very well, then--you shall learn who he is.

Johan: Do not speak!

Bernick: Not a word more!

Rorlund: If I did not, I should be unworthy to serve a community of whose morals I have been appointed a guardian, and should be acting most unjustifiably towards this young girl, in whose upbringing I have taken a material part, and who is to me--

Johan: Take care what you are doing!

Rorlund: She shall know! Dina, this is the man who was the cause of all your mother's misery and shame.

Bernick: Mr. Rorlund--?

Dina: He! (TO JOHAN.) Is this true?

Johan: Karsten, you answer.

Bernick: Not a word more! Do not let us say another word about it today.

Dina: Then it is true.

Rorlund: Yes, it is true. And more than that, this fellow--whom you were going to trust--did not run away from home empty-handed; ask him about old Mrs. Bernick's cash-box.... Mr. Bernick can bear witness to that!

Lona: Liar

Bernick: Ah!

Mrs. Bernick: My God! my God!

Johan (rushing at RORLUND with uplifted arm): And you dare to--

Lona (restraining him): Do not strike him, Johan!

Rorlund: That is right, assault me! But the truth will out; and it is the truth--Mr. Bernick has admitted it--and the whole town knows it. Now, Dina, you know him. (A short silence.)

Johan (softly, grasping BERNICK by the arm): Karsten, Karsten, what have you done?

Mrs. Bernick (in tears): Oh, Karsten, to think that I should have mixed you up in all this disgrace!

Sandstad (coming in hurriedly from the right, and calling out, with his hand still on the door-handle): You positively must come now, Mr. Bernick. The fate of the whole railway is hanging by a thread.

Bernick (abstractedly): What is it? What have I to--

Lona (earnestly and with emphasis): You have to go and be a pillar of society, brother-in-law.

Sandstad: Yes, come along; we need the full weight of your moral excellence on our side.

Johan (aside, to BERNICK): Karsten, we will have a talk about this tomorrow. (Goes out through the garden. BERNICK, looking half dazed, goes out to the right with SANDSTAD.)

ACT III

(SCENE--The same room. BERNICK, with a cane in his hand and evidently in a great rage, comes out of the farther room on the left, leaving the door half-open behind him.)

Bernick (speaking to his wife, who is in the other room): There! I have given it him in earnest now; I don't think he will forget that thrashing! What do you say?--And I say that you are an injudicious mother! You make excuses for him, and countenance any sort of rascality on his part--Not rascality? What do you call it, then? Slipping out of the house at night, going out in a fishing boat, staying away till well on in the day, and giving me such a horrible fright when I have so much to worry me! And then the young scamp has the audacity to threaten that he will run away! Just let him try!--You? No, very likely; you don't trouble yourself much about what happens to him. I really believe that if he were to get killed--! Oh, really? Well, I have work to leave behind me in the world; I have no fancy for being left childless--Now, do not raise objections, Betty; it shall be as I say--he is confined to the house. (Listens.) Hush; do not let any one notice anything. (KRAP comes in from the right.)

Krap: Can you spare me a moment, Mr. Bernick?

Bernick (throwing away the cane): Certainly, certainly. Have you come from the yard?

Krap: Yes. Ahem--!

Bernick: Well? Nothing wrong with the "Palm Tree," I hope?

Krap: The "Palm Tree" can sail tomorrow, but

Bernick: It is the "Indian Girl," then? I had a suspicion that that obstinate fellow--

Krap: The "Indian Girl" can sail tomorrow, too; but I am sure she will not get very far.

Bernick: What do you mean?

Krap: Excuse me, sir; that door is standing ajar, and I think there is some one in the other room--

Bernick (shutting the door): There, then! But what is this that no one else must hear?

Krap: Just this--that I believe Aune intends to let the "Indian Girl" go to the bottom with every mother's son on board.

Bernick: Good God!--what makes you think that?

Krap: I cannot account for it any other way, sir.

Bernick: Well, tell me as briefly as you can

Krap: I will. You know yourself how slowly the work has gone on in the yard since we got the new machines and the new inexperienced hands?

Bernick: Yes, yes.

Krap: But this morning, when I went down there, I noticed that the repairs to the American boat had made extraordinary progress; the great hole in the bottom--the rotten patch, you know--

Bernick: Yes, yes--what about it?

Krap: Was completely repaired--to all appearance at any rate, covered up--looked as good as new. I heard that Aune himself had been working at it by lantern light the whole night.

Bernick: Yes, yes--well?

Krap: I turned it over in my head for a bit; the hands were away at their breakfast, so I found an opportunity to have a look around the boat, both outside and in, without anyone seeing me. I had a job to get down to the bottom through the cargo, but I learned the truth. There is something very suspicious going on, Mr. Bernick.

Bernick: I cannot believe it, Krap. I cannot and will not believe such a thing of Aune.

Krap: I am very sorry--but it is the simple truth. Something very suspicious is going on. No new timbers put in, as far as I could see, only stopped up and tinkered at, and covered over with sailcloth and tar-paulins and that sort of thing--an absolute fraud. The "Indian Girl" will never get to New York; she will go to the bottom like a cracked pot.

Bernick: This is most horrible! But what can be his object, do you suppose?

Krap: Probably he wants to bring the machines into discredit--wants to take his revenge--wants to force you to take the old hands on again.

Bernick: And to do this he is willing to sacrifice the lives of all on board.

Krap: He said the other day that there were no men on board the "Indian Girl"--only wild beasts.

Bernick: Yes, but--apart from that--has he no regard for the great loss of capital it would mean?

Krap: Aune does not look upon capital with a very friendly eye, Mr. Bernick.

Bernick: That is perfectly true; he is an agitator and a fomenter of discontent; but such an unscrupulous thing as this--Look here, Krap; you must look into the matter once more. Not a word of it to any one. The blame will fall on our yard if any one hears anything of it.

Krap: Of course, but--

Bernick: When the hands are away at their dinner you must manage to get down there again; I must have absolute certainty about it.

Krap: You shall, sir; but, excuse me, what do you propose to do?

Bernick: Report the affair, naturally. We cannot, of course, let ourselves become accomplices in such a crime. I could not have such a thing on my conscience. Moreover, it will make a good impression, both on the press and on the public in general, if it is seen that I set all personal interests aside and let justice take its course.

Krap: Quite true, Mr. Bernick.

Bernick: But first of all I must be absolutely certain. And meanwhile, do not breathe a word of it.

Krap: Not a word, sir. And you shall have your certainty. (Goes out through the garden and down the street.)

Bernick (half aloud): Shocking!--But no, it is impossible! Inconceivable!

(As he turns to go into his room, HILMAR comes in from the right.)

Hilmar: Good morning, Karsten. Let me congratulate you on your triumph at the Commercial Association yesterday.

Bernick: Thank you.

Hilmar: It was a brilliant triumph, I hear; the triumph of intelligent public spirit over selfishness and prejudice--something like a raid of French troops on the Kabyles. It is astonishing that after that unpleasant scene here, you could--

Bernick: Yes, yes--quite so.

Hilmar: But the decisive battle has not been fought yet.

Bernick: In the matter of the railway, do you mean?

Hilmar: Yes; I suppose you know the trouble that Hammer is brewing?

Bernick (anxiously): No, what is that?

Hilmar: Oh, he is greatly taken up with the rumour that is going around, and is preparing to dish up an article about it.

Bernick: What rumour?

Hilmar: About the extensive purchase of property along the branch line, of course.

Bernick: What? Is there such a rumour as that going about?

Hilmar: It is all over the town. I heard it at the club when I looked in there. They say that one of our lawyers has quietly bought up, on commission, all the forest land, all the mining land, all the waterfalls--

Bernick: Don't they say whom it was for?

Hilmar: At the club they thought it must be for some company, not connected with this town, that has got a hint of the scheme you have in hand, and has made haste to buy before the price of these properties went up. Isn't it villainous?--ugh!

Bernick: Villainous?

Hilmar: Yes, to have strangers putting their fingers into our pie--and one of our own local lawyers lending himself to such a thing! And now it will be outsiders that will get all the profits!

Bernick: But, after all, it is only an idle rumour.

Hilmar: Meanwhile people are believing it, and tomorrow or the next day, I have no doubt Hammer will nail it to the counter as a fact. There is a general sense of exasperation in the town already. I heard several people say that if the rumour were confirmed they would take their names off the subscription lists.

Bernick: Impossible!

Hilmar: Is it? Why do you suppose these mercenary-minded creatures were so willing to go into the undertaking with you? Don't you suppose they have scented profit for themselves--

Bernick: It is impossible, I am sure; there is so much public spirit in our little community--

Hilmar: In our community? Of course you are a confirmed optimist, and so you judge others by yourself. But I, who am a tolerably experienced observer--! There isn't a single soul in the place--excepting ourselves, of course--not a single soul in the place who holds up the banner of the Ideal. (Goes towards the verandah.) Ugh, I can see them there--

Bernick: See whom?

Hilmar: Our two friends from America. (Looks out to the right.) And who is that they are walking with? As I am alive, if it is not the captain of the "Indian Girl." Ugh!

Bernick: What can they want with him?

Hilmar. Oh, he is just the right company for them. He looks as if he had been a slave-dealer or a pirate; and who knows what the other two may have been doing all these years.

Bernick: Let me tell you that it is grossly unjust to think such things about them.

Hilmar: Yes--you are an optimist. But here they are, bearing down upon us again; so I will get away while there is time. (Goes towards the door on the left. LONA comes in from the right.)

Lona: Oh, Hilmar, am I driving you away?

Hilmar: Not at all; I am in rather a hurry; I want to have a word with Betty. (Goes into the farthest room on the left.)

Bernick (after a moment's silence): Well, Lona?

Lona: Yes?

Bernick: What do you think of me today?

Lona: The same as I did yesterday. A lie more or less--

Bernick: I must enlighten you about it. Where has Johan gone?

Lona: He is coming; he had to see a man first.

Bernick: After what you heard yesterday, you will understand that my whole life will be ruined if the truth comes to light.

Lona: I can understand that.

Bernick: Of course, it stands to reason that I was not guilty of the crime there was so much talk about here.

Lona: That stands to reason. But who was the thief?

Bernick: There was no thief. There was no money stolen--not a penny.

Lona: How is that?

Bernick: Not a penny, I tell you.

Lona: But those rumours? How did that shameful rumour get about that Johan--

Bernick: Lona, I think I can speak to you as I could to no one else. I will conceal nothing from you. I was partly to blame for spreading the rumour.

Lona: You? You could act in that way towards a man who for your sake--!

Bernick: Do not condemn me without bearing in mind how things stood at that time. I told you about it yesterday. I came home and found my mother involved in a mesh of injudicious undertakings; we had all manner of bad luck--it seemed as if misfortunes were raining upon us, and our house was on the verge of ruin. I was half reckless and half in despair. Lona, I believe it was mainly to deaden my thoughts that I let myself drift into that entanglement that ended in Johan's going away.

Lona: Hm--

Bernick: You can well imagine how every kind of rumour was set on foot after you and he had gone. People began to say that it was not his first piece of folly--that Dorf had received a large sum of money to hold his tongue and go away; other people said that she had received it. At the same time it was obvious that our house was finding it difficult to meet its obligations. What was more natural than that scandal-mongers should find some connection between these two rumours? And as the woman remained here, living in poverty, people declared that he had taken the money with him to America; and every time rumour mentioned the sum, it grew larger.

Lona: And you, Karsten--?

Bernick: I grasped at the rumour like a drowning man at a straw.

Lona: You helped to spread it?

Bernick: I did not contradict it. Our creditors had begun to be pressing, and I had the task of keeping them quiet. The result was the dissipating of any suspicion as to the stability of the firm; people said that we had been hit by a temporary piece of ill-luck--that all that was necessary was that they should not press us--only give us time and every creditor would be paid in full.

Lona: And every creditor was paid in full?

Bernick: Yes, Lona, that rumour saved our house and made me the man I now am.

Lona: That is to say, a lie has made you the man you now are.

Bernick: Whom did it injure at the time? It was Johan's intention never to come back.

Lona: You ask whom it injured. Look into your own heart, and tell me if it has not injured you.

Bernick: Look into any man's heart you please, and you will always find, in every one, at least one black spot which he has to keep concealed.

Lona: And you call yourselves pillars of society!

Bernick: Society has none better.

Lona: And of what consequence is it whether such a society be propped up or not? What does it all consist of? Show and lies--and nothing else. Here are you, the first man in the town, living in grandeur and luxury, powerful and respected--you, who have branded an innocent man as a criminal.

Bernick: Do you suppose I am not deeply conscious of the wrong I have done him? And do you suppose I am not ready to make amends to him for it?

Lona: How? By speaking out?

Bernick: Would you have the heart to insist on that?

Lona: What else can make amends for such a wrong?

Bernick: I am rich, Lona; Johan can demand any sum he pleases.

Lona: Yes, offer him money, and you will hear what he will say.

Bernick: Do you know what he intends to do?

Lona: No; since yesterday he has been dumb. He looks as if this had made a grown man of him all at once.

Bernick: I must talk to him.

Lona: Here he comes. (JOHAN comes in from the right.)

Bernick (going towards hint): Johan--!

Johan (motioning him away): Listen to me first. Yesterday morning I gave you my word that I would hold my tongue.

Bernick: You did.

Johan: But then I did not know--

Bernick: Johan, only let me say a word or two to explain the circumstances--

Johan: It is unnecessary; I understand the circumstances perfectly. The firm was in a dangerous position at the time; I had gone off, and you had my defenceless name and reputation at your mercy. Well, I do not blame you so very much for what you did; we were young and thoughtless in those days. But now I have need of the truth, and now you must speak.

Bernick: And just now I have need of all my reputation for morality, and therefore I cannot speak.

Johan: I don't take much account of the false reports you spread about me; it is the other thing that you must take the blame of. I shall make Dina my wife, and here--here in your town--I mean to settle down and live with her.

Lona: Is that what you mean to do?

Bernick: With Dina? Dina as your wife?--in this town?

Johan: Yes, here and nowhere else. I mean to stay here to defy all these liars and slanderers. But before I can win her, you must exonerate me.

Bernick: Have you considered that, if I confess to the one thing, it will inevitably mean making myself responsible for the other as well? You will say that I can show by our books that nothing dishonest happened? But I cannot; our books were not so accurately kept in those days. And even if I could, what good would it do? Should I not in any case be pointed at as the man who had once saved himself by an untruth, and for fifteen years had allowed that untruth and all its consequences to stand without having raised a finger to demolish it? You do not know our community very much, or you would realise that it would ruin me utterly.

Johan: I can only tell you that I mean to make Mrs. Dorf's daughter my wife, and live with her in this town.

Bernick (wiping the perspiration from his forehead): Listen to me, Johan--and you too, Lona. The circumstances I am in just now are quite exceptional. I am situated in such a way that if you aim this blow at me you will not only destroy me, but will also destroy a great future, rich in blessings, that lies before the community which, after all, was the home of your childhood.

Johan: And if I do not aim this blow at you, I shall be destroying all my future happiness with my own hand.

Lona: Go on, Karsten.

Bernick: I will tell you, then. It is mixed up with the railway project, and the whole thing is not quite so simple as you think. I suppose you have heard that last year there was some talk of a railway line along the coast? Many influential people backed up the idea--people in the town and the suburbs, and especially the press; but I managed to get the proposal quashed, on the ground that it would have injured our steamboat trade along the coast.

Lona: Have you any interest in the steamboat trade?

Bernick: Yes. But no one ventured to suspect me on that account; my honoured name fully protected me from that. For the matter of that, I could have stood the loss; but the place could not have stood it. So the inland line was decided upon. As soon as that was done, I assured myself--without saying anything about it--that a branch line could be laid to the town.

Lona: Why did you say nothing about it, Karsten?

Bernick: Have you heard the rumours of extensive buying up of forest lands, mines and waterfalls--?

Johan: Yes, apparently it is some company from another part of the country.

Bernick: As these properties are situated at present, they are as good as valueless to their owners, who are scattered about the neighbourhood; they have therefore been sold comparatively cheap. If the purchaser had waited till the branch line began to be talked of, the proprietors would have asked exorbitant prices.

Lona: Well--what then?

Bernick: Now I am going to tell you something that can be construed in different ways--a thing to which, in our community, a man could only confess provided he had an untarnished and honoured name to take his stand upon.

Lona: Well?

Bernick: It is I that have bought up the whole of them.

Lona: You?

Johan: On your own account?

Bernick: On my own account. If the branch line becomes an accomplished fact, I am a millionaire; if it does not, I am ruined.

Lona: It is a big risk, Karsten.

Bernick: I have risked my whole fortune on it.

Lona: I am not thinking of your fortune; but if it comes to light that--

Bernick. Yes, that is the critical part of it. With the unblemished and honoured name I have hitherto borne, I can take the whole thing upon my shoulders, carry it through, and say to my fellow-citizens: "See, I have taken this risk for the good of the community."

Lona: Of the community?

Bernick: Yes; and not a soul will doubt my motives.

Lona: Then some of those concerned in it have acted more openly-- without any secret motives or considerations.

Bernick: Who?

Lona: Why, of course, Rummel and Sandstad and Vigeland.

Bernick: To get them on my side I was obliged to let them into the secret.

Lona: And they?

Bernick: They have stipulated for a fifth part of the profits as their share.

Lona: Oh, these pillars of society.

Bernick: And isn't it society itself that forces us to use these under-handed means? What would have happened if I had not acted se-cretly? Everybody would have wanted to have a hand in the under-taking; the whole thing would have been divided up, mismanaged and bungled. There is not a single man in the town except myself who is capable of directing so big an affair as this will be. In this country, almost without exception, it is only foreigners who have settled here who have the aptitude for big business schemes. That is the reason why my conscience acquits me in the matter. It is only in my hands that these properties can become a real blessing to the many who have to make their daily bread.

Lona: I believe you are right there, Karsten.

Johan: But I have no concern with the many, and my life's happiness is at stake.

Bernick: The welfare of your native place is also at stake. If things come out which cast reflections on my earlier conduct, then all my opponents will fall upon me with united vigour. A youthful folly is never allowed to be forgotten in our community. They would go through the whole of my previous life, bring up a thousand little inci-dents in it, interpret and explain them in the light of what has been revealed; they would crush me under the weight of rumours and slan-ders. I should be obliged to abandon the railway scheme; and, if I take my hand off that, it will come to nothing, and I shall be ruined and my life as a citizen will be over.

Lona: Johan, after what we have just heard, you must go away from here and hold your tongue.

Bernick: Yes, yes, Johan--you must!

Johan: Yes, I will go away, and I will hold my tongue; but I shall come back, and then I shall speak.

Bernick: Stay over there, Johan; hold your tongue, and I am willing to share with you--

Johan: Keep your money, but give me back my name and reputation.

Bernick: And sacrifice my own!

Johan: You and your community must get out of that the best way you can. I must and shall win Dina for my wife. And therefore, I am going to sail tomorrow in the "Indian Girl"--

Bernick: In the "Indian Girl"?

Johan: Yes. The captain has promised to take me. I shall go over to America, as I say; I shall sell my farm, and set my affairs in order. In two months I shall be back.

Bernick: And then you will speak?

Johan: Then the guilty man must take his guilt on himself.

Bernick: Have you forgotten that, if I do that, I must also take on myself guilt that is not mine?

Johan: Who is it that for the last fifteen years has benefited by that shameful rumour?

Bernick: You will drive me to desperation! Well, if you speak, I shall deny everything! I shall say it is a plot against me--that you have come here to blackmail me!

Lona: For shame, Karsten!

Bernick: I am a desperate man, I tell you, and I shall fight for my life. I shall deny everything--everything!

Johan: I have your two letters. I found them in my box among my other papers. This morning I read them again; they are plain enough.

Bernick: And will you make them public?

Johan: If it becomes necessary.

Bernick: And you will be back here in two months?

Johan: I hope so. The wind is fair. In three weeks I shall be in New York--if the "Indian Girl" does not go to the bottom.

Bernick (with a start): Go to the bottom? Why should the "Indian Girl" go to the bottom?

Johan: Quite so--why should she?

Bernick (scarcely audibly): Go to the bottom?

Johan: Well, Karsten, now you know what is before you. You must find your own way out. Good-bye! You can say good-bye to Betty for me, although she has not treated me like a sister. But I must see Martha. She shall tell Dina---; she shall promise me--(Goes out through the farther door on the left.)

Bernick (to himself): The "Indian Girl"--? (Quickly.) Lona, you must prevent that!

Lona: You see for yourself, Karsten--I have no influence over him any longer. (Follows JOHAN into the other room.)

Bernick (a prey to uneasy thoughts): Go to the bottom--?

(AUNE comes in from the right.)

Aune: Excuse me, sir, but if it is convenient--

Bernick (turning round angrily): What do you want?

Aune: To know if I may ask you a question, sir.

Bernick: Be quick about it, then. What is it?

Aune: I wanted to ask if I am to consider it as certain--absolutely certain--that I should be dismissed from the yard if the "Indian Girl" were not ready to sail tomorrow?

Bernick: What do you mean? The ship is ready to sail?

Aune: Yes--it is. But suppose it were not, should I be discharged?

Bernick: What is the use of asking such idle questions?

Aune: Only that I should like to know, sir. Will you answer me that?--should I be discharged?

Bernick: Am I in the habit of keeping my word or not?

Aune: Then tomorrow I should have lost the position I hold in my house and among those near and dear to me--lost my influence over men of my own class--lost all opportunity of doing anything for the cause of the poorer and needier members of the community?

Bernick: Aune, we have discussed all that before.

Aune: Quite so--then the "Indian Girl" will sail.

(A short silence.)

Bernick: Look here--it is impossible for me to have my eyes everywhere--I cannot be answerable for everything. You can give me your assurance, I suppose, that the repairs have been satisfactorily carried out?

Aune: You gave me very short grace, Mr. Bernick.

Bernick: But I understand you to warrant the repairs?

Aune: The weather is fine, and it is summer.

(Another pause.)

Bernick: Have you anything else to say to me?

Aune: I think not, sir.

Bernick: Then--the "Indian Girl" will sail...

Aune: Tomorrow?

Bernick: Yes.

Aune: Very good. (Bows and goes out. BERNICK stands for a moment irresolute; then walks quickly towards the door, as if to call AUNE back; but stops, hesitatingly, with his hand on the door-handle. At that moment the door is opened from without, and KRAP comes in.)

Krap (in a low voice): Aha, he has been here. Has he confessed?

Bernick: Hm--; have you discovered anything?

84

Krap: What need of that, sir? Could you not see the evil conscience looking out of the man's eyes?

Bernick: Nonsense--such things don't show. Have you discovered anything, I want to know?

Krap: I could not manage it; I was too late. They had already begun hauling the ship out of the dock. But their very haste in doing that plainly shows that--

Bernick: It shows nothing. Has the inspection taken place, then?

Krap: Of course; but--

Bernick: There, you see! And of course they found nothing to complain of?

Krap: Mr. Bernick, you know very well how much this inspection means, especially in a yard that has such a good name as ours has.

Bernick: No matter--it takes all responsibility off us.

Krap: But, sir, could you really not tell from Aune's manner that--?

Bernick: Aune has completely reassured me, let me tell you.

Krap: And let me tell you, sir, that I am morally certain that--

Bernick: What does this mean, Krap? I see plainly enough that you want to get your knife into this man; but if you want to attack him, you must find some other occasion. You know how important it is to me--or, I should say, to the owners--that the "Indian Girl" should sail to-morrow.

Krap: Very well--so be it; but if ever we hear of that ship again--hm!

(VIGELAND comes in from the right.)

Vigeland: I wish you a very good morning, Mr. Bernick. Have you a moment to spare?

Bernick: At your service, Mr. Vigeland.

Vigeland: I only want to know if you are also of opinion that the "Palm Tree" should sail tomorrow?

Bernick: Certainly; I thought that was quite settled.

Vigeland: Well, the captain came to me just now and told me that storm signals have been hoisted.

Bernick: Oh! Are we to expect a storm?

Vigeland: A stiff breeze, at all events; but not a contrary wind--just the opposite.

Bernick: Hm--well, what do you say?

Vigeland: I say, as I said to the captain, that the "Palm Tree" is in the hands of Providence. Besides, they are only going across the North Sea at first; and in England, freights are running tolerably high just now, so that--

Bernick: Yes, it would probably mean a loss for us if we waited.

Vigeland: Besides, she is a stout ship, and fully insured as well. It is more risky, now, for the "Indian Girl"--

Bernick: What do you mean?

Vigeland: She sails tomorrow, too.

Bernick: Yes, the owners have been in such a hurry, and, besides--

Vigeland: Well, if that old hulk can venture out--and with such a crew, into the bargain--it would be a disgrace to us if we--

Bernick: Quite so. I presume you have the ship's papers with you.

Vigeland: Yes, here they are.

Bernick: Good; then will you go in with Mr. Krap?

Krap: Will you come in here, sir, and we will dispose of them at once.

Vigeland: Thank you.--And the issue we leave in the hands of the Almighty, Mr. Bernick. (Goes with KRAP into BERNICK'S room. RORLUND comes up from the garden.)

Rorlund: At home at this time of day, Mr. Bernick?

Bernick (lost in thought): As you see.

Rorlund: It was really on your wife's account I came. I thought she might be in need of a word of comfort.

Bernick: Very likely she is. But I want to have a little talk with you, too.

Rorlund: With the greatest of pleasure, Mr. Bernick. But what is the matter with you? You look quite pale and upset.

Bernick: Really? Do I? Well, what else could you expect--a man so loaded with responsibilities as I am? There is all my own big business--and now the planning of this railway.--But tell me something, Mr. Rorlund, let me put a question to you.

Rorlund: With pleasure, Mr. Bernick.

Bernick: It is about a thought that has occurred to me. Suppose a man is face to face with an undertaking which will concern the welfare of thousands, and suppose it should be necessary to make a sacrifice of one--?

Rorlund: What do you mean?

Bernick: For example, suppose a man were thinking of starting a large factory. He knows for certain--because all his experience has taught him so--that sooner or later a toll of human life will be exacted in the working of that factory.

Rorlund: Yes, that is only too probable.

Bernick: Or, say a man embarks on a mining enterprise. He takes into his service fathers of families and young men in the first flush of their youth. Is it not quite safe to predict that all of them will not come out of it alive?

Rorlund: Yes, unhappily that is quite true.

Bernick: Well--a man in that position will know beforehand that the undertaking he proposes to start must undoubtedly, at some time or other, mean a loss of human life. But the undertaking itself is for the public good; for every man's life that it costs, it will undoubtedly promote the welfare of many hundreds.

Rorlund: Ah, you are thinking of the railway--of all the dangerous excavating and blasting, and that sort of thing--

Bernick: Yes--quite so--I am thinking of the railway. And, besides, the coming of the railway will mean the starting of factories and mines. But do not think, nevertheless--

Rorlund: My dear Mr. Bernick, you are almost over-conscientious. What I think is that, if you place the affair in the hands of Providence--

Bernick: Yes--exactly; Providence--

Rorlund: You are blameless in the matter. Go on and build your railway hopefully.

Bernick: Yes, but now I will put a special instance to you. Suppose a charge of blasting-powder had to be exploded in a dangerous place, and that unless it were exploded the line could not be constructed? Suppose the engineer knew that it would cost the life of the workman who lit the fuse, but that it had to be lit, and that it was the engineer's duty to send a workman to do it?

Rorlund: Hm--

Bernick: I know what you will say. It would be a splendid thing if the engineer took the match himself and went and lit the fuse. But that is out of the question, so he must sacrifice a workman.

Rorlund: That is a thing no engineer here would ever do.

Bernick: No engineer in the bigger countries would think twice about doing it.

Rorlund: In the bigger countries? No, I can quite believe it. In those depraved and unprincipled communities.

Bernick: Oh, there is a good deal to be said for those communities.

Rorlund: Can you say that?--you, who yourself--

Bernick: In the bigger communities a man finds space to carry out a valuable project--finds the courage to make some sacrifice in a great cause; but here, a man is cramped by all kinds of petty considerations and scruples.

Rorlund: Is human life a petty consideration?

Bernick: When that human life threatens the welfare of thousands.

Rorlund: But you are suggesting cases that are quite inconceivable, Mr. Bernick! I do not understand you at all today. And you quote the bigger countries--well, what do they think of human life there? They look upon it simply as part of the capital they have to use. But we look at things from a somewhat different moral standpoint, I should hope. Look at our respected shipping industry! Can you name a single one of our ship-owners who would sacrifice a human life for the sake of paltry gain? And then think of those scoundrels in the bigger countries, who for the sake of profit send out freights in one unseaworthy ship after another--

Bernick: I am not talking of unseaworthy ships!

Rorlund: But I am, Mr. Bernick.

Bernick: Yes, but to what purpose? They have nothing to do with the question--Oh, these small, timid considerations! If a General from this country were to take his men under fire and some of them were shot, I suppose he would have sleepless nights after it! It is not so in other countries. You should bear what that fellow in there says--

Rorlund: He? Who? The American--?

Bernick: Yes. You should hear how in America--

Rorlund: He, in there? And you did not tell me? I shall at once--

Bernick: It is no use; you won't be able to do anything with him.

Rorlund: We shall see. Ah, here he comes. (JOHAN comes in from the other room.)

Johan (talking back through the open door): Yes, yes, Dina--as you please; but I do not mean to give you up, all the same. I shall come back, and then everything will come right between us.

Rorlund: Excuse me, but what did you mean by that? What is it you propose to do?

Johan: I propose that that young girl, before whom you blackened my character yesterday, shall become my wife.

Rorlund: Your wife? And can you really suppose that--?

Johan: I mean to marry her.

Rorlund: Well, then you shall know the truth. (Goes to the half-open door.) Mrs. Bernick, will you be so kind as to come and be a witness-- and you too, Miss Martha. And let Dina come. (Sees LONA at the door.) Ah, you here too?

Lona: Shall I come too?

Rorlund: As many as you please--the more the better.

Bernick: What are you going to do? (LONA, MRS. BERNICK, MAR-THA, DINA and HILMAR come in from the other room.)

Mrs. Bernick: Mr. Rorlund, I have tried my hardest, but I cannot prevent him...

Rorlund: I shall prevent him, Mrs. Bernick. Dina, you are a thoughtless girl, but I do not blame you so greatly. You have too long lacked the necessary moral support that should have sustained you. I blame myself for not having afforded you that support.

Dina: You mustn't speak now!

Mrs. Bernick: What is it?

Rorlund: It is now that I must speak, Dina, although your conduct yesterday and today has made it ten times more difficult for me. But all other considerations must give way to the necessity for saving you. You remember that I gave you my word; you remember what you promised you would answer when I judged that the right time had come. Now I dare not hesitate any longer, and therefore--. (Turns to JOHAN.) This young girl, whom you are persecuting, is my betrothed.

Mrs. Bernick: What?

Bernick: Dina!

Johan: She? Your--?

Martha: No, no, Dina!

Lona: It is a lie!

Johan: Dina--is this man speaking the truth?

Dina (after a short pause): Yes.

Rorlund: I hope this has rendered all your arts of seduction powerless. The step I have determined to take for Dina's good, I now wish openly proclaimed to every one. I cherish the certain hope that it will not be misinterpreted. And now, Mrs. Bernick, I think it will be best for us to take her away from here, and try to bring back peace and tranquillity to her mind.

Mrs. Bernick: Yes, come with me. Oh, Dina--what a lucky girl you are! (Takes DINA Out to the left; RORLUND follows them.)

Martha: Good-bye, Johan! (Goes out.)

Hilmar (at the verandah door): Hm--I really must say...

Lona (who has followed DINA with her eyes, to JOHAN): Don't be downhearted, my boy! I shall stay here and keep my eye on the parson. (Goes out to the right.)

Bernick: Johan, you won't sail in the "Indian Girl" now?

Johan: Indeed I shall.

Bernick: But you won't come back?

Johan: I am coming back.

Bernick: After this? What have you to do here after this?

Johan: Revenge myself on you all; crush as many of you as I can. (Goes out to the right. VIGELAND and KRAP come in from BERNICK'S room.)

Vigeland: There, now the papers are in order, Mr. Bernick.

Bernick: Good, good.

Krap (in a low voice): And I suppose it is settled that the "Indian Girl" is to sail tomorrow?

Bernick: Yes. (Goes into his room. VIGELAND and KRAP go out to the right. HILMAR is just going after them, when OLAF puts his head carefully out of the door on the left.)

Olaf: Uncle! Uncle Hilmar!

Hilmar: Ugh, is it you? Why don't you stay upstairs? You know you are confined to the house.

Olaf (coming a step or two nearer): Hush! Uncle Hilmar, have you heard the news?

Hilmar: Yes, I have heard that you got a thrashing today.

Olaf (looking threateningly towards his father's room): He shan't thrash me any more. But have you heard that Uncle Johan is going to sail tomorrow with the Americans?

Hilmar: What has that got to do with you? You had better run upstairs again.

Olaf: Perhaps I shall be going for a buffalo hunt, too, one of these days, uncle.

Hilmar: Rubbish! A coward like you--

Olaf: Yes--just you wait! You will learn something tomorrow!

Hilmar: Duffer! (Goes out through the garden. OLAF runs into the room again and shuts the door, as he sees KRAP coming in from the right.)

Krap (going to the door of BERNICK'S room and opening it slightly): Excuse my bothering you again, Mr. Bernick; but there is a tremendous storm blowing up. (Waits a moment, but there is no answer.) Is the "Indian Girl" to sail, for all that? (After a short pause, the following answer is heard.)

Bernick (from his room): The "Indian Girl" is to sail, for all that.

(KRAP Shuts the door and goes out again to the right.)

ACT IV

(SCENE--The same room. The work-table has been taken away. It is a stormy evening and already dusk. Darkness sets in as the following scene is in progress. A man-servant is lighting the chandelier; two maids bring in pots of flowers, lamps and candles, which they place on tables and stands along the walls. RUMMEL, in dress clothes, with gloves and a white tie, is standing in the room giving instructions to the servants.)

Rummel: Only every other candle, Jacob. It must not look as if it were arranged for the occasion--it has to come as a surprise, you know. And all these flowers--? Oh, well, let them be; it will probably look as if they stood there everyday. (BERNICK comes out of his room.)

Bernick (stopping at the door): What does this mean?

Rummel: Oh dear, is it you? (To the servants.) Yes, you might leave us for the present. (The servants go out.)

Bernick: But, Rummel, what is the meaning of this?

Rummel: It means that the proudest moment of your life has come. A procession of his fellow citizens is coming to do honour to the first man of the town.

Bernick: What!

Rummel: In procession--with banners and a band! We ought to have had torches too; but we did not like to risk that in this stormy weather. There will be illuminations--and that always sounds well in the newspapers.

Bernick: Listen, Rummel--I won't have anything to do with this.

Rummel: But it is too late now; they will be here in half-an-hour.

Bernick: But why did you not tell me about this before?

Rummel: Just because I was afraid you would raise objections to it. But I consulted your wife; she allowed me to take charge of the arrangements, while she looks after the refreshments.

Bernick (listening): What is that noise? Are they coming already? I fancy I hear singing.

Rummel (going to the verandah door): Singing? Oh, that is only the Americans. The "Indian Girl" is being towed out.

Bernick: Towed out? Oh, yes. No, Rummel, I cannot this evening; I am not well.

Rummel: You certainly do look bad. But you must pull yourself together; devil take it--you must! Sandstad and Vigeland and I all attach the greatest importance to carrying this thing through. We have got to crush our opponents under the weight of as complete an expression of public opinion as possible. Rumours are getting about the town; our announcement about the purchase of the property cannot be withheld any longer. It is imperative that this very evening--after songs and speeches, amidst the clink of glasses--in a word, in an ebullient atmosphere of festivity--you should inform them of the risk you have incurred for the good of the community. In such an ebullient atmosphere of festivity--as I just now described it--you can do an astonishing lot with the people here. But you must have that atmosphere, or the thing won't go.

Bernick: Yes, yes.

Rummel: And especially when so delicate and ticklish a point has to be negotiated. Well, thank goodness, you have a name that will be a tower of strength, Bernick. But listen now; we must make our arrangements, to some extent. Mr. Hilmar Tonnesen has written an ode to you. It begins very charmingly with the words: "Raise the Ideal's banner high!" And Mr. Rorlund has undertaken the task of making the speech of the evening. Of course you must reply to that.

Bernick: I cannot tonight, Rummel. Couldn't you--?

Rummel: It is impossible, however willing I might be; because, as you can imagine, his speech will be especially addressed to you. Of course it is possible he may say a word or two about the rest of us; I have spoken to Vigeland and Sandstad about it. Our idea is that, in replying, you should propose the toast of "Prosperity to our Community"; Sandstad will say a few words on the subject of harmonious relations between the different strata of society; then Vigeland will express the hope that this new undertaking may not disturb the sound moral basis upon which our community stands; and I propose, in a few suitable words, to refer to the ladies, whose work for the community, though more inconspicuous, is far from being without its importance. But you are not listening to me.

Bernick: Yes--indeed I am. But, tell me, do you think there is a very heavy sea running outside?

Rummel: Why, are you nervous about the "Palm Tree"? She is fully insured, you know.

Bernick: Yes, she is insured; but--

Rummel: And in good repair--and that is the main thing.

Bernick: Hm--. Supposing anything does happen to a ship, it doesn't follow that human life will be in danger, does it? The ship and the cargo may be lost--and one might lose one's boxes and papers--

Rummel: Good Lord--boxes and papers are not of much consequence.

Bernick: Not of much consequence! No, no; I only meant--. Hush--I hear voices again.

Rummel: It is on board the "Palm Tree."

(VIGELAND comes in from the right.)

Vigeland: Yes, they are just towing the "Palm Tree" out. Good evening, Mr. Bernick.

Bernick: And you, as a seafaring man, are still of opinion that--

Vigeland: I put my trust in Providence, Mr. Bernick. Moreover, I have been on board myself and distributed a few small tracts which I hope may carry a blessing with them.

(SANDSTAD and KRAP come in from the right.)

Sandstad (to some one at the door): Well, if that gets through all right, anything will. (Comes in.) Ah, good evening, good evening!

Bernick: Is anything the matter, Krap?

Krap: I say nothing, Mr. Bernick.

Sandstad: The entire crew of the "Indian Girl" are drunk; I will stake my reputation on it that they won't come out of it alive. (LONA comes in from the right.)

Lona: Ah, now I can say his good-byes for him.

Bernick: Is he on board already?

Lona: He will be directly, at any rate. We parted outside the hotel.

Bernick: And he persists in his intention?

Lona: As firm as a rock.

Rummel (who is fumbling at the window): Confound these new-fangled contrivances; I cannot get the curtains drawn.

Lona: Do you want them drawn? I thought, on the contrary--

Rummel: Yes, drawn at first, Miss Hessel. You know what is in the wind, I suppose?

Lona: Yes. Let me help you. (Takes hold of the cords.) I will draw down the curtains on my brother-in-law--though I would much rather draw them up.

Rummel: You can do that too, later on. When the garden is filled with a surging crowd, then the curtains shall be drawn back, and they will be able to look in upon a surprised and happy family. Citizens' lives should be such that they can live in glass houses! (BERNICK opens his mouth, as though he were going to say something; but he turns hurriedly away and goes into his room.)

Rummel: Come along, let us have a final consultation. Come in, too, Mr. Krap; you must assist us with information on one or two points of detail. (All the men go into BERNICK'S room. LONA has drawn the curtains over the windows, and is just going to do the same over the open glass door, when OLAF jumps down from the room above on to the garden steps; he has a wrap over his shoulders and a bundle in his hand.)

Lona: Bless me, child, how you frightened me!

Olaf (hiding his bundle): Hush, aunt!

Lona: Did you jump out of the window? Where are you going?

Olaf: Hush!--don't say anything. I want to go to Uncle Johan--only on to the quay, you know--only to say goodbye to him. Good-night, aunt! (Runs out through the garden.)

Lona: No--stop! Olaf--Olaf!

(JOHAN, dressed for his journey, with a bag over his shoulder, comes warily in by the door on the right.)

Johan: Lona!

Lona (turning round): What! Back again?

Johan: I have still a few minutes. I must see her once more; we cannot part like this. (The farther door on the left opens, and MARTHA and DINA, both with cloaks on, and the latter carrying a small travelling bag in her hand, come in.)

Dina: Let me go to him! Let me go to him!

Martha: Yes, you shall go to him, Dina!

Dina: There he is!

Johan: Dina!

Dina: Take me with you!

Johan: What--!

Lona: You mean it?

Dina: Yes, take me with you. The other has written to me that he means to announce to everyone this evening.

Johan: Dina--you do not love him?

Dina: I have never loved the man! I would rather drown myself in the fjord than be engaged to him! Oh, how he humiliated me yesterday with his condescending manner! How clear he made it that he felt he was lifting up a poor despised creature to his own level! I do not mean to be despised any longer. I mean to go away. May I go with you?

Johan: Yes, yes--a thousand times, yes!

Dina: I will not be a burden to you long. Only help me to get over there; help me to go the right way about things at first.

Johan: Hurrah, it is all right after all, Dina!

Lona (pointing to BERNICK'S door): Hush!--gently, gently!

Johan: Dina, I shall look after you.

Dina: I am not going to let you do that. I mean to look after myself; over there, I am sure I can do that. Only let me get away from here. Oh, these women!--you don't know--they have written to me today, too--exhorting me to realise my good fortune--impressing on me how magnanimous he has been. Tomorrow, and every day afterwards, they would be watching me to see if I were making myself worthy of it all. I am sick and tired of all this goodness!

Johan: Tell me, Dina--is that the only reason you are coming away? Am I nothing to you?

Dina: Yes, Johan, you are more to me than any one else in the world.

Johan: Oh, Dina--!

Dina: Every one here tells me I ought to hate and detest you--that it is my duty; but I cannot see that it is my duty, and shall never be able to.

Lona: No more you shall, my dear!

Martha: No, indeed you shall not; and that is why you shall go with him as his wife.

Johan: Yes, yes!

Lona: What? Give me a kiss, Martha. I never expected that from you!

Martha: No, I dare say not; I would not have expected it myself. But I was bound to break out some time! Ah, what we suffer under the tyranny of habit and custom! Make a stand against that, Dina. Be his wife. Let me see you defy all this convention.

Johan: What is your answer, Dina?

Dina: Yes, I will be your wife.

Johan: Dina!

Dina: But first of all I want to work--to make something of myself--as you have done. I am not going to be merely a thing that is taken.

Lona: Quite right--that is the way.

Johan: Very well; I shall wait and hope--

Lona: And win, my boy! But now you must get on board!

Johan: Yes, on board! Ah, Lona, my dear sister, just one word with you. Look here-- (He takes her into the background and talks hurriedly to her.)

Martha: Dina, you lucky girl, let me look at you, and kiss you once more--for the last time.

Dina: Not for the last time; no, my darling aunt, we shall meet again.

Martha: Never! Promise me, Dina, never to come back! (Grasps her hands and looks at her.) Now go to your happiness, my dear child--across the sea. How often, in my schoolroom, I have yearned to be over there! It must be beautiful; the skies are loftier than here--a freer air plays about your head--

Dina: Oh, Aunt Martha, some day you will follow us.

Martha: I? Never--never. I have my little vocation here, and now I really believe I can live to the full the life that I ought.

Dina: I cannot imagine being parted from you.

Martha: Ah, one can part from much, Dina. (Kisses her.) But I hope you may never experience that, my sweet child. Promise me to make him happy.

Dina: I will promise nothing; I hate promises; things must happen as they will.

Martha: Yes, yes, that is true; only remain what you are--true and faithful to yourself.

Dina: I will, aunt.

100

Lona (putting into her pocket some papers that JOHAN has given her): Splendid, splendid, my dear boy. But now you must be off.

Johan: Yes, we have no time to waste now. Goodbye, Lona, and thank you for all your love. Goodbye, Martha, and thank you, too, for your loyal friendship.

Martha: Goodbye, Johan! Goodbye, Dina! And may you be happy all your lives! (She and LONA hurry them to the door at the back. JOHAN and DINA go quickly down the steps and through the garden. LONA shuts the door and draws the curtains over it.)

Lona: Now we are alone, Martha. You have lost her and I him.

Martha: You--lost him?

Lona: Oh, I had already half lost him over there. The boy was longing to stand on his own feet; that was why I pretended to be suffering from homesickness.

Martha: So that was it? Ah, then I understand why you came. But he will want you back, Lona.

Lona: An old step-sister--what use will he have for her now? Men break many very dear ties to win their happiness.

Martha: That sometimes is so.

Lona: But we two will stick together, Martha.

Martha: Can I be anything to you?

Lona: Who more so? We two foster-sisters--haven't we both lost our children? Now we are alone.

Martha: Yes, alone. And therefore, you ought to know this too--I loved him more than anything in the world.

Lona: Martha! (Grasps her by the arm.) Is that true?

Martha: All my existence lies in those words. I have loved him and waited for him. Every summer I waited for him to come. And then he came--but he had no eyes for me.

Lona: You loved him! And it was you yourself that put his happiness into his hands.

Martha: Ought I not to be the one to put his happiness into his hands, since I loved him? Yes, I have loved him. All my life has been for him, ever since he went away. What reason had I to hope, you mean? Oh, I think I had some reason, all the same. But when he came back--then it seemed as if everything had been wiped out of his memory. He had no eyes for me.

Lona: It was Dina that overshadowed you, Martha?

Martha: And it is a good thing she did. At the time he went away, we were of the same age; but when I saw him again--oh, that dreadful moment!--I realised that now I was ten years older than he. He had gone out into the bright sparkling sunshine, and breathed in youth and health with every breath; and here I sat meanwhile, spinning and spinning--

Lona: Spinning the thread of his happiness, Martha.

Martha: Yes, it was a golden thread I spun. No bitterness! We have been two good sisters to him, haven't we, Lona?

Lona (throwing her arms round her): Martha!

(BERNICK comes in from his room.)

Bernick (to the other men, who are in his room): Yes, yes, arrange it any way you please. When the time comes, I shall be able to--. (Shuts the door.) Ah, you are here. Look here, Martha--I think you had better change your dress; and tell Betty to do the same. I don't want anything elaborate, of course--something homely, but neat. But you must make haste.

Lona: And a bright, cheerful face, Martha; your eyes must look happy.

Bernick: Olaf is to come downstairs too; I will have him beside me.

Lona: Hm! Olaf.

Martha: I will give Betty your message. (Goes out by the farther door on the left.)

102

Lona: Well, the great and solemn moment is at hand.

Bernick (walking uneasily up and down): Yes, it is.

Lona: At such a moment I should think a man would feel proud and happy.

Bernick (looking at her): Hm!

Lona: I hear the whole town is to be illuminated.

Bernick: Yes, they have some idea of that sort.

Lona: All the different clubs will assemble with their banners--your name will blaze out in letters of fire--tonight the telegraph will flash the news to every part of the country: "In the bosom of his happy family, Mr. Bernick received the homage of his fellow citizens, as one of the pillars of society."

Bernick: That is so; and they will begin to cheer outside, and the crowd will shout in front of my house until I shall be obliged to go out and bow to them and thank them.

Lona: Obliged to?

Bernick. Do you suppose I shall feel happy at that moment?

Lona: No, I don't suppose you will feel so very happy.

Bernick: Lona, you despise me.

Lona: Not yet.

Bernick: And you have no right to; no right to despise me! Lona, you can have no idea how utterly alone I stand in this cramped and stunted community--where I have had, year after year, to stifle my ambition for a fuller life. My work may seem many-sided, but what have I really accomplished? Odds and ends--scraps. They would not stand anything else here. If I were to go a step in advance of the opinions and views that are current at the moment, I should lose all my influence. Do you know what we are--we who are looked upon as pillars of society? We are nothing more, nor less, than the tools of society.

Lona: Why have you only begun to realise that now?

Bernick: Because I have been thinking a great deal lately--since you came back--and this evening I have thought more seriously than ever before. Oh, Lona, why did not I really know you then--in the old days, I mean?

Lona: And if you had?

Bernick: I should never have let you go; and, if I had had you, I should not be in the position I am in tonight.

Lona: And do you never consider what she might have been to you-- she whom you chose in my place?

Bernick: I know, at all events, that she has been nothing to me of what I needed.

Lona: Because you have never shared your interests with her; because you have never allowed her full and frank exchange of thoughts with you; because you have allowed her to be borne under by self-reproach for the shame you cast upon one who was dear to her.

Bernick: Yes, yes; it all comes from lying and deceit.

Lona: Then why not break with all this lying and deceit?

Bernick: Now? It is too late now, Lona.

Lona: Karsten, tell me--what gratification does all this show and deception bring you?

Bernick: It brings me none. I must disappear someday, and all this community of bunglers with me. But a generation is growing up that will follow us; it is my son that I work for--I am providing a career for him. There will come a time when truth will enter into the life of the community, and on that foundation he shall build up a happier existence than his father.

Lona: With a lie at the bottom of it all? Consider what sort of an inheritance it is that you are leaving to your son.

Bernick (in tones of suppressed despair): It is a thousand times worse than you think. But surely some day the curse must be lifted; and yet- -nevertheless--. (Vehemently.) How could I bring all this upon my own head! Still, it is done now; I must go on with it now. You shall

104

not succeed in crushing me! (HILMAR comes in hurriedly and agitatedly from the right, with an open letter in his hand.)

Hilmar: But this is--Betty, Betty.

Bernick: What is the matter? Are they coming already?

Hilmar: No, no--but I must speak to some one immediately. (Goes out through the farther door on the left.)

Lona: Karsten, you talk about our having come here to crush you. So let me tell you what sort of stuff this prodigal son, whom your moral community shuns as if he had the plague, is made of. He can do without any of you--for he is away now.

Bernick: But he said he meant to come back

Lona: Johan will never come back. He is gone for good, and Dina with him.

Bernick: Never come back?--and Dina with him?

Lona: Yes, to be his wife. That is how these two strike your virtuous community in the face, just as I did once--but never mind that.

Bernick: Gone--and she too--in the "Indian Girl"--

Lona: No; he would not trust so precious a freight to that rascally crew. Johan and Dina are on the "Palm Tree."

Bernick: Ah! Then it is all in vain-- (Goes hurriedly to the door of his room, opens it and calls in.) Krap, stop the "Indian Girl"--she must not sail tonight!

Krap (from within): The "Indian Girl" is already standing out to sea, Mr. Bernick.

Bernick (shutting the door and speaking faintly): Too late--and all to no purpose--

Lona: What do you mean?

Bernick: Nothing, nothing. Leave me alone!

Lona: Hm!--look here, Karsten. Johan was good enough to say that he entrusted to me the good name and reputation that he once lent to you, and also the good name that you stole from him while he was away. Johan will hold his tongue; and I can act just as I please in the matter. See, I have two letters in my hand.

Bernick: You have got them! And you mean now--this very evening-perhaps when the procession comes--

Lona: I did not come back here to betray you, but to stir your conscience so that you should speak of your own free will. I did not succeed in doing that--so you must remain as you are, with your life founded upon a lie. Look, I am tearing your two letters in pieces. Take the wretched things--there you are. Now there is no evidence against you, Karsten. You are safe now; be happy, too--if you can.

Bernick (much moved): Lona--why did you not do that sooner! Now it is too late; life no longer seems good to me; I cannot live on after today.

Lona: What has happened?

Bernick: Do not ask me--But I must live on, nevertheless! I will live--for Olaf's sake. He shall make amends for everything--expiate everything.

Lona: Karsten--! (HILMAR comes hurriedly back.)

Hilmar: I cannot find anyone; they are all out--even Betty!

Bernick: What is the matter with you?

Hilmar: I daren't tell you.

Bernick: What is it? You must tell me!

Hilmar: Very well--Olaf has run away, on board the "Indian Girl."

Bernick (stumbling back): Olaf--on board the "Indian Girl"! No, no!

Lona: Yes, he is! Now I understand--I saw him jump out of the window.

Bernick (calls in through the door of his room in a despairing voice): Krap, stop the "Indian Girl" at any cost!

Krap: It is impossible, sir. How can you suppose--?

106

Bernick: We must stop her; Olaf is on board!

Krap: What!

Rummel (coming out of BERNICK'S room): Olaf, run away? Impossible!

Sandstad (following him): He will be sent back with the pilot, Mr. Bernick.

Hilmar: No, no; he has written to me. (Shows the letter.) He says he means to hide among the cargo till they are in the open sea.

Bernick: I shall never see him again!

Rummel: What nonsense!--a good strong ship, newly repaired...

Vigeland (who has followed the others out of BERNICK'S room): And in your own yard, Mr. Bernick!

Bernick: I shall never see him again, I tell you. I have lost him, Lona; and--I see it now--he never was really mine. (Listens.) What is that?

Rummel: Music. The procession must be coming.

Bernick. I cannot take any part in it--I will not.

Rummel: What are you thinking of! That is impossible.

Sandstad: Impossible, Mr. Bernick; think what you have at stake.

Bernick: What does it all matter to me now? What have I to work for now?

Rummel: Can you ask? You have us and the community.

Vigeland: Quite true.

Sandstad: And surely, Mr. Bernick, you have not forgotten that we--.(MARTHA comes in through the farther door to the left. Music is heard in the distance, down the street.)

Martha: The procession is just coming, but Betty is not in the house. I don't understand where she--

Bernick: Not in the house! There, you see, Lona--no support to me, either in gladness or in sorrow.

Rummel: Draw back the curtains! Come and help me, Mr. Krap--and you, Mr. Sandstad. It is a thousand pities that the family should not be united just now; it is quite contrary to the program. (They draw back all the curtains. The whole street is seen to be illuminated. Opposite the house is a large transparency, bearing the words: "Long live Karsten Bernick, Pillar of our Society ")

Bernick (shrinking back): Take all that away! I don't want to see it! Put it out, put it out!

Rummel: Excuse me, Mr. Bernick, but are you not well?

Martha: What is the matter with him, Lona?

Lona: Hush! (Whispers to her.)

Bernick: Take away those mocking words, I tell you! Can't you see that all these lights are grinning at us?

Rummel: Well, really, I must confess--

Bernick: Oh, how could you understand--! But I, I--! It is all like candles in a dead-room!

Rummel: Well, let me tell you that you are taking the thing a great deal too seriously.

Sandstad: The boy will enjoy a trip across the Atlantic, and then you will have him back.

Vigeland: Only put your trust in the Almighty, Mr. Bernick.

Rummel: And in the vessel, Bernick; it is not likely to sink, I know.

Krap: Hm--

Rummel: Now if it were one of those floating coffins that one hears are sent out by men in the bigger countries--

Bernick: I am sure my hair must be turning grey--

(MRS. BERNICK comes in from the garden, with a shawl thrown over her head.)

Mrs. Bernick: Karsten, Karsten, do you know--?

108

Bernick: Yes. I know; but you--you, who see nothing that is going on--you, who have no mother's eyes for your son--!

Mrs. Bernick: Listen to me, do!

Bernick: Why did you not look after him? Now I have lost him. Give him back to me, if you can.

Mrs. Bernick: I can! I have got him.

Bernick: You have got him!

The Men: Ah!

Hilmar: Yes, I thought so.

Martha: You have got him back, Karsten.

Lona: Yes--make him your own, now.

Bernick: You have got him! Is that true? Where is he?

Mrs. Bernick: I shall not tell you, till you have forgiven him.

Bernick: Forgiven! But how did you know--?

Mrs. Bernick: Do you not think a mother sees? I was in mortal fear of your getting to know anything about it. Some words he let fall yesterday--and then his room was empty, and his knapsack and clothes missing...

Bernick: Yes, yes?

Mrs. Bernick: I ran, and got hold of Aune; we went out in his boat; the American ship was on the point of sailing. Thank God, we were in time--got on board--searched the hold--found him! Oh, Karsten, you must not punish him!

Bernick: Betty!

Mrs. Bernick: Nor Aune, either!

Bernick: Aune? What do you know about him? Is the "Indian Girl" under sail again?

Mrs. Bernick: No, that is just it.

Bernick: Speak, speak!

Mrs. Bernick: Aune was just as agitated as I was; the search took us some time; it had grown dark, and the pilot made objections; and so Aune took upon himself--in your name--

Bernick: Well?

Mrs. Bernick: To stop the ship's sailing till tomorrow.

Krap: Hm--

Bernick: Oh, how glad I am!

Mrs. Bernick: You are not angry?

Bernick: I cannot tell you how glad I am, Betty

Rummel: You really take things far too seriously.

Hilmar: Oh yes, as soon as it is a question of a little struggle with the elements--ugh!

Krap (going to the window): The procession is just coming through your garden gate, Mr. Bernick.

Bernick: Yes, they can come now.

Rummel: The whole garden is full of people.

Sandstad: The whole street is crammed.

Rummel: The whole town is afoot, Bernick. It really is a moment that makes one proud.

Vigeland: Let us take it in a humble spirit, Mr. Rummel.

Rummel: All the banners are out! What a procession! Here comes the committee with Mr. Rorlund at their head.

Bernick: Yes, let them come in!

Rummel: But, Bernick--in your present agitated frame of mind--

Bernick: Well, what?

Rummel: I am quite willing to speak instead of you, if you like.

Bernick: No, thank you; I will speak for myself tonight.

Rummel: But are you sure you know what to say?

Bernick: Yes, make your mind easy, Rummel--I know now what to say.

(The music grows louder. The verandah door is opened. RORLUND comes in, at the head of the Committee, escorted by a couple of hired waiters, who carry a covered basket. They are followed by townspeople of all classes, as many as can get into the room. An apparently endless crowd of people, waving banners and flags, are visible in the garden and the street.)

Rorlund: Mr. Bernick! I see, from the surprise depicted upon your face, that it is as unexpected guests that we are intruding upon your happy family circle and your peaceful fireside, where we find you surrounded by honoured and energetic fellow citizens and friends. But it is our hearts that have bidden us come to offer you our homage--not for the first time, it is true, but for the first time on such a comprehensive scale. We have on many occasions given you our thanks for the broad moral foundation upon which you have, so to speak, reared the edifice of our community. On this occasion we offer our homage especially to the clear-sighted, indefatigable, unselfish--nay, self-sacrificing citizen who has taken the initiative in an undertaking which, we are assured on all sides, will give a powerful impetus to the temporal prosperity and welfare of our community.

Voices: Bravo, bravo!

Rorlund: You, sir, have for many years been a shining example in our midst. This is not the place for me to speak of your family life, which has been a model to us all; still less to enlarge upon your unblemished personal character. Such topics belong to the stillness of a man's own chamber, not to a festal occasion such as this! I am here to speak of your public life as a citizen, as it lies open to all men's eyes. Well-equipped vessels sail away from your shipyard and carry our flag far and wide over the seas. A numerous and happy band of workmen look up to you as to a father. By calling new branches of industry into existence, you have laid the foundations of the welfare of hundreds of families. In a word--you are, in the fullest sense of the term, the main-stay of our community.

Voices: Hear, hear! Bravo!

Rorlund: And, sir, it is just that disinterestedness, which colours all your conduct, that is so beneficial to our community--more so than words can express--and especially at the present moment. You are now on the point of procuring for us what I have no hesitation in call-ing bluntly by its prosaic name--a railway!

Voices: Bravo, bravo!

Rorlund: But it would seem as though the undertaking were beset by certain difficulties, the outcome of narrow and selfish considerations.

Voices: Hear, hear!

Rorlund: For the fact has come to light that certain individuals, who do not belong to our community, have stolen a march upon the hard-working citizens of this place, and have laid hands on certain sources of profit which by rights should have fallen to the share of our town.

Voices: That's right! Hear, hear!

Rorlund: This regrettable fact has naturally come to your knowledge also, Mr. Bernick. But it has not had the slightest effect in deterring you from proceeding steadily with your project, well knowing that a patriotic man should not solely take local interests into consideration.

Voices: Oh!--No, no!--Yes, yes!

Rorlund: It is to such a man--to the patriot citizen, whose character we all should emulate--that we bring our homage this evening. May your undertaking grow to be a real and lasting source of good fortune to this community! It is true enough that a railway may be the means of our exposing ourselves to the incursion of pernicious influences from without; but it gives us also the means of quickly expelling them from within. For even we, at the present time, cannot boast of being entirely free from the danger of such outside influences; but as we have, on this very evening--if rumour is to be believed--fortunately got rid of certain elements of that nature, sooner than was to be expected--

Voices: Order, order!

Rorlund:--I regard the occurrence as a happy omen for our undertaking. My alluding to such a thing at such a moment only emphasises the fact that the house in which we are now standing is one where the claims of morality are esteemed even above ties of family.

Voices: Hear, hear! Bravo!

Bernick (at the same moment): Allow me--

Rorlund: I have only a few more words to say, Mr. Bernick. What you have done for your native place we all know has not been done with any underlying idea of its bringing tangible profit to yourself. But, nevertheless, you must not refuse to accept a slight token of grateful appreciation at the hands of your fellow-citizens--least of all at this important moment when, according to the assurances of practical men, we are standing on the threshold of a new era.

Voices: Bravo! Hear, hear!

(RORLUND signs to the servants, who bring forward the basket. During the following speech, members of the Committee take out and present the various objects mentioned.)

Rorlund: And so, Mr. Bernick, we have the pleasure of presenting you with this silver coffee-service. Let it grace your board when in the future, as so often in the past, we have the happiness of being assembled under your hospitable roof. You, too, gentlemen, who have so generously seconded the leader of our community, we ask to accept a small souvenir. This silver goblet is for you, Mr. Rummel. Many a time have you, amidst the clink of glasses, defended the interests of your fellow-citizens in well-chosen words; may you often find similar worthy opportunities to raise and empty this goblet in some patriotic toast! To you, Mr. Sandstad, I present this album containing photographs of your fellow-citizens. Your well-known and conspicuous liberality has put you in the pleasant position of being able to number your friends amongst all classes of society. And to you, Mr. Vigeland, I have to offer this book of Family Devotions, printed on vellum and handsomely bound, to grace your study table. The mellowing influence of time has led you to take an earnest view of life; your zeal in carrying out your daily duties has, for a long period of years, been purified and enobled by thoughts of higher and holier things. (Turns to the crowd.) And now, friends, three cheers for Mr. Bernick and his fellow-workers! Three cheers for the Pillars of our Society!

The whole crowd: Bernick! Pillars of Society! Hurrah-hurrah-hurrah!

Lona: I congratulate you, brother-in-law.

(An expectant hush follows.)

Bernick (speaking seriously and slowly): Fellow citizens--your spokesman said just now that tonight we are standing on the threshold of a new era. I hope that will prove to be the case. But before that can come to pass, we must lay fast hold of truth--truth which, till tonight, has been altogether and in all circumstances a stranger to this community of ours. (Astonishment among the audience.) To that end, I must begin by deprecating the praises with which you, Mr. Rorlund, according to custom on such occasions, have overwhelmed me. I do not deserve them; because, until today, my actions have by no means been disinterested. Even though I may not always have aimed at pecuniary profit, I at all events recognise now that a craving for power, influence and position has been the moving spirit of most of my actions.

Rummel (half aloud): What next!

Bernick: Standing before my fellow citizens, I do not reproach myself for that; because I still think I am entitled to a place in the front rank of our capable men of affairs.

Voices: Yes, yes, yes!

Bernick: But what I charge myself with is that I have so often been weak enough to resort to deceitfulness, because I knew and feared the tendency of the community to espy unclean motives behind everything a prominent man here undertakes. And now I am coming to a point which will illustrate that.

Rummel (uneasily): Hm-hm!

Bernick: There have been rumours of extensive purchases of property outside the town. These purchases have been made by me--by me

114

alone, and by no one else. (Murmurs are heard: "What does he say?--He?--Bernick?") The properties are, for the time being, in my hands. Naturally I have confided in my fellow-workers, Mr. Rummel, Mr. Vigeland and Mr. Sandstad, and we are all agreed that--

Rummel: It is not true! Prove it--prove it!

Vigeland: We are not all agreed about anything!

Sandstad: Well, really I must say--!

Bernick: That is quite true--we are not yet agreed upon the matter I was going to mention. But I confidently hope that these three gentlemen will agree with me when I announce to you that I have tonight come to the decision that these properties shall be exploited as a company of which the shares shall be offered for public subscription; any one that wishes can take shares.

Voices: Hurrah! Three cheers for Bernick!

Rummel (in a low voice, to BERNICK): This is the basest treachery--!

Sandstad (also in an undertone): So you have been fooling us!

Vigeland: Well, then, devil take--! Good Lord, what am I saying?

(Cheers are heard without.)

Bernick: Silence, gentlemen. I have no right to this homage you offer me; because the decision I have just come to does not represent what was my first intention. My intention was to keep the whole thing for myself; and, even now, I am of opinion that these properties would be worked to best advantage if they remained in one man's hands. But you are at liberty to choose. If you wish it, I am willing to administer them to the best of my abilities.

Voices: Yes, yes, yes!

Bernick: But, first of all, my fellow townsmen must know me thoroughly. And let each man seek to know himself thoroughly, too; and so let it really come to pass that tonight we begin a new era. The old era--with its affectation, its hypocrisy and its emptiness, its pretence of virtue and its miserable fear of public opinion--shall be for us like a museum, open for purposes of instruction; and to that museum we will present--shall we not, gentlemen?--the coffee service, and the goblet, and the album, and the Family Devotions printed on vellum, and handsomely bound.

Rummel: Oh, of course.

Vigeland (muttering): If you have taken everything else, then--

Sandstad: By all means.

Bernick: And now for the principal reckoning I have to make with the community. Mr. Rorlund said that certain pernicious elements had left us this evening. I can add what you do not yet know. The man referred to did not go away alone; with him, to become his wife, went--

Lona (loudly): Dina Dorf!

Rorlund: What?

Mrs. Bernick: What? (Great commotion.)

Rorlund: Fled? Run away--with him! Impossible!

Bernick: To become his wife, Mr. Rorlund. And I will add more. (In a low voice, to his wife.) Betty, be strong to bear what is coming. (Aloud.) This is what I have to say: hats off to that man, for he has nobly taken another's guilt upon his shoulders. My friends, I want to have done with falsehood; it has very nearly poisoned every fibre of my being. You shall know all. Fifteen years ago, I was the guilty man.

Mrs. Bernick (softly and tremblingly): Karsten!

Martha (similarly): Ah, Johan--!

Lona: Now at last you have found yourself!

(Speechless consternation among the audience.)

Bernick: Yes, friends, I was the guilty one, and he went away. The vile and lying rumours that were spread abroad afterwards, it is beyond human power to refute now; but I have no right to complain of that. For fifteen years I have climbed up the ladder of success by the help of those rumours; whether now they are to cast me down again, or not, each of you must decide in his own mind.

Rorlund: What a thunderbolt! Our leading citizen--! (In a low voice, to BETTY.) How sorry I am for you, Mrs. Bernick!

Hilmar: What a confession! Well, I must say--!

Bernick: But come to no decision tonight. I entreat every one to go home--to collect his thoughts--to look into his own heart. When once more you can think calmly, then it will be seen whether I have lost or won by speaking out. Goodbye! I have still much--very much--to repent of; but that concerns my own conscience only. Good night! Take away all these signs of rejoicing. We must all feel that they are out of place here.

Rorlund: That they certainly are. (In an undertone to MRS. BERNICK.) Run away! So then she was completely unworthy of me. (Louder, to the Committee.) Yes, gentlemen, after this I think we had better disperse as quietly as possible.

Hilmar: How, after this, any one is to manage to hold the Ideal's banner high--Ugh!

(Meantime the news has been whispered from mouth to mouth. The crowd gradually disperses from the garden. RUMMEL, SANDSTAD and VIGELAND go out, arguing eagerly but in a low voice. HILMAR slinks away to the right. When silence is restored, there only remain in the room BERNICK, MRS. BERNICK, MARTHA, LONA and KRAP.)

Bernick: Betty, can you forgive me?

Mrs. Bernick (looking at him with a smile): Do you know, Karsten, that you have opened out for me the happiest prospect I have had for many a year?

Bernick: How?

Mrs. Bernick: For many years, I have felt that once you were mine and that I had lost you. Now I know that you never have been mine yet; but I shall win you.

Bernick (folding her in his arms): Oh, Betty, you have won me. It was through Lona that I first learned really to know you. But now let Olaf come to me.

Mrs. Bernick: Yes, you shall have him now. Mr. Krap--! (Talks softly to KRAP in the background. He goes out by the garden door. During what follows, the illuminations and lights in the houses are gradually extinguished.)

Bernick (in a low voice): Thank you, Lona--you have saved what was best in me--and for me.

Lona: Do you suppose I wanted to do anything else?

Bernick: Yes, was that so--or not? I cannot quite make you out.

Lona: Hm--

Bernick: Then it was not hatred? Not revenge? Why did you come back, then?

Lona: Old friendship does not rust.

Bernick: Lona!

Lona: When Johan told me about the lie, I swore to myself that the hero of my youth should stand free and true.

Bernick: What a wretch I am!--and how little I have deserved it of you!

Lona. Oh, if we women always looked for what we deserve, Karsten--!

(AUNE comes in with OLAF from the garden.)

Bernick (going to meet them): Olaf!

Olaf: Father, I promise I will never do it again--

Bernick: Never run away?

Olaf: Yes, yes, I promise you, father.

Bernick: And I promise you, you shall never have reason to. For the future you shall be allowed to grow up, not as the heir to my life's work, but as one who has his own life's work before him.

Olaf: And shall I be allowed to be what I like, when I grow up?

Bernick: Yes.

Olaf. Oh, thank you! Then I won't be a pillar of society.

Bernick: No? Why not?

Olaf: No--I think it must be so dull.

Bernick: You shall be yourself, Olaf; the rest may take care of itself--And you, Aune...

Aune: I know, Mr. Bernick; I am dismissed.

Bernick: We remain together, Aune; and forgive me.

Aune: What? The ship has not sailed tonight.

Bernick: Nor will it sail tomorrow, either. I gave you too short grace. It must be looked to more thoroughly.

Aune: It shall, Mr. Bernick--and with the new machines!

Bernick: By all means--but thoroughly and conscientiously. There are many among us who need thorough and conscientious repairs, Aune. Well, good night.

Aune: Good-night, sir--and thank you, thank you. (Goes out.)

Mrs. Bernick: Now they are all gone.

Bernick: And we are alone. My name is not shining in letters of fire any longer; all the lights in the windows are out.

Lona: Would you wish them lit again?

Bernick: Not for anything in the world. Where have I been! You would be

horrified if you knew. I feel now as if I had come back to my right senses, after being poisoned. But I feel this that I can be young and healthy again. Oh, come nearer--come closer round me. Come, Betty! Come, Olaf, my boy! And you, Martha--it seems to me as if I had never seen you all these years.

Lona: No, I can believe that. Your community is a community of bachelor souls; you do not see women.

Bernick: That is quite true; and for that very reason--this is a bargain, Lona--you must not leave Betty and me.

Mrs. Bernick: No, Lona, you must not.

Lona: No, how could I have the heart to go away and leave you young people who are just setting up housekeeping? Am I not your foster-mother? You and I, Martha, the two old aunts-- What are you looking at?

Martha: Look how the sky is clearing, and how light it is over the sea. The "Palm Tree" is going to be lucky.

Lona: It carries its good luck on board.

Bernick: And we--we have a long earnest day of work ahead of us; I most of all. But let it come; only keep close round me you true, loyal women. I have learned this too, in these last few days; it is you women that are the pillars of society.

Lona: You have learned a poor sort of wisdom, then, brother-in-law. (Lays her hand firmly upon his shoulder.) No, my friend; the spirit of truth and the spirit of freedom--they are the pillars of society.